GLOWING PRAISE FOR
CHRISTINA CRAWFORD'S *SURVIVOR*

"Christina Crawford has seen the heart of darkness—and survived...."   — *Rocky Mountain News*

"The author of *Mommie Dearest* ... hits her stride with this strong account of her simultaneous tragedies....One closes this fine, moving read with great respect for Christina Crawford."   — *Kirkus*

"This is a passage book. It is the personal interior journey of an adult, emotionally damaged by child abuse, who still searches to discover hope and a deep sense of belonging....Inspiring."
     — *Baton Rouge Sunday Magazine*

"The author of *Mommie Dearest* has survived calamities that would sink a lesser person....Her candor and humor make *Survivor* notable." — *Boston Herald*

"A survivor's tale....That first book was a landmark in discussing the horrible secret of child abuse. It propelled Christina Crawford into the spotlight as a champion for abused youngsters and for the psychologically scarred grown-ups they become....*Survivor* [has] a novel's ability to draw readers into the experience."   — *Chattanooga News-Free Press*

"Riveting!"   — *Charleston Sunday Post/Courier*

Also by Christina Crawford

MOMMIE DEAREST
BLACK WIDOW

Survivor

CHRISTINA CRAWFORD

JOVE BOOKS, NEW YORK

This Jove book contains the complete
text of the original hardcover edition.
It has been completely reset in a typeface
designed for easy reading, and was printed
from new film.

SURVIVOR

A Jove Book / published by arrangement with
Donald I. Fine, Inc.

PRINTING HISTORY
Donald I. Fine edition / October 1988
Published in Canada by General Publishing Company, Limited
Jove edition / February 1990

ISBN: 0-515-10299-7

Jove Books are published by The Berkley Publishing Group,
200 Madison Avenue, New York, New York 10016.
The name "JOVE" and the "J" logo
are trademarks belonging to Jove Publications, Inc.

PRINTED IN THE UNITED STATES OF AMERICA

10 9 8 7 6 5 4 3 2 1

THIS BOOK IS DEDICATED WITH LOVE TO THOSE FRIENDS AND TEACHERS IN ALL REALITIES WHO HAVE SEEN ME THROUGH PAST YEARS OF PAINFUL CHAOS SO THAT WE MAY SHARE TOGETHER THIS PRESENT TIME OF HEALING AND HAPPINESS.

CONTENTS

CONTENTS

Survivor

DREAMS

WHEN I WAS a little girl, I looked up at the night stars and made wishes on them. The night stars became the guardians of my secret dreams. They twinkled down at my hopeful face, so filled with belief and trust. In that shimmering brightness, I imagined acknowledgment, perhaps even recognition, from the universe, of the small, green-eyed, silver-haired child standing alone in a twilight garden, sending skyward her hopes and dreams.

The future seemed to be personified in those stars, their shapes and the symbols to which they bore witness.

The formal symbols were meaningless to me, but the mystery . . . the reliability . . . were comforting and hopeful.

No other person in my young world ever heard my dreams. I told them only to the stars. I had never learned the process of trusting in others, so the repository of my faith, my trust, my hope, remained where it had initially found safety—skyward, in the universe.

My dreams were never as fragile as my ability to believe

that someday they would come true. In fact, the dreams themselves were strong and healthy.

In my dreams, all I wanted was to live to grow up, then to find someone to love me and finally, to be able to be recognized and respected as an independent woman in a world I knew nothing about.

It was a very long way from there to now. Day by day gremlins and demons beset my journey toward the fulfillment of my dreams. Despair sucked energy from me and I floundered time and time again.

Yet it was persistence that finally brought me close, not yet to my secrets stored for a lifetime in the skyward stars of my childhood longings, but close to a possibility, a possible reality that momentarily helped soothe the yearning, the longing, the searing emptiness, the disappointment. These possible realities were the adult moments of closeness, of marriage and family, of holiday laughter replacing holiday tears, of a fragile sense of belonging instead of a lifetime of wandering terrified and therefore ultradefensive.

Still, I didn't know that I didn't know anything about real relationships, about sharing, about personal boundaries, about trust, about being centered, about loving myself or anyone close. Maybe I thought that everyone was born with the same natural ability to develop into healthy maturity and that it only required the right opportunity.

For me, part of that opportunity was a long-term romantic relationship. On Valentine's Day in 1976, David and I were married.

I had waited thirty-six years to share my dreams with someone and I melded myself to him for assurance that I had chosen a trustworthy recipient. It was important for me to believe in him as holder of the trust in order for me to continue believing in the dream at all.

Being married was part of the dream. His young son was another part of the same dream. The first dream was called family.

Now that I had created a family, I felt that I belonged somewhere. I was anchored through the dream to these two, to protect and care for them, to educate and defend them.

These beliefs, it seemed to me, were what one offered to loved ones, and my demonstration of these beliefs was to become a fierce loyalty and protectiveness. Some of my fierceness also became blind.

Another of my dreams, the second dream, was being believed, being understood, being validated as a whole person ... as me.

It never dawned on me that instead of the dream coming true, a nightmare would be in store for me. That nightmare would be a replay of my childhood, for my sense of self was rocked once again with the publication of my book *Mommie Dearest*. I had thought that since I was now an adult, writing for an audience whose eyes were opened by Watergate, my historical, experiential autobiography would be believed, even if only as a glimpse of the private person hidden carefully by the public image.

Of course I had expected the material to be viewed as unconventional, perhaps even sensational, but never did I imagine it would ignite years of soul-shattering controversy that would threaten my life and my sanity.

Who could have known? I wrote my book as the story of a child trying desperately to survive in a relationship with a powerful, insecure, consuming woman who was my mother but who was known to the public only as a film screen fantasy from many years past. It was a relationship based on prolonged sadistic punishment alternating with jealously possessive love. Who could have known that my individual and solitary struggle for survival would suddenly shock the world by exposing it to millions of counterparts?

Who could have known in advance that the book would land a direct hit on one of our last cultural taboos?

Who would have dreamed that it would become a mirror held up to reflect the private moments of all parent-child relationships when they involve violence, whether the violence is physical or psychological?

Who would have imagined that it would expose a social cancer of tragic proportions?

How could I have envisioned that my physical and emotional survival would have to be defended, explained, justified thousands of times in the media, then privately by millions of others who knew I was telling the truth because my book revealed truths from their own childhoods?

Certainly not I. Not my husband nor my young stepson. Not even the publisher.

I found myself catapulted from private life into a storm of controversy as the hurricane of public opinion blew across the country in the fall of 1978.

To say we were all caught unprepared is an understatement.

And in the process, parts of the dreams were shattered.

Yet today, I find myself once again in the role of being my own historian.

I seek to capture all the different realities through which my life has taken me; to capture these realities with the passages of my word-nets, as if chasing reluctant butterflies, so that I may stick these word-nets onto paper and share the myriad realities with you.

Why? Because *who* I am has been so variously interpreted. Why? Because of public mirrors and past errors. Why? Because of the concept of the phantasma, the illusive dream and the magic lantern picture show of our minds. Why? Because of a place where dreams and illusions and different realities meet and where change is a constant fixture of life. Why? Because I learned that lost is a place, too!

MAPS AND TRANSITIONS

THE JOURNEY FROM the known to the unknown is perhaps an eternal one, across all times, generations and cultures.

This book is about the life process of transition, of transformation, rebirth. This book is about being a survivor, no matter what events life holds in store.

For most of the journey I was without a map, without enough information, without people to guide me.

So, it is also a journey of faltering. It is a life of contradictions, of controversy, of extremes, of chaos. In the process, my journey has taken me through anger, rage, passion, driving ambition, despair, near death, and finally, miraculously, into rebirth—a transformative life experience.

In the earliest days of world exploration, those who were willing to take risks, those who listened to the wisdom of others, those who were able to remember the information, survived. They were the ones eventually entrusted to be the makers of maps.

With those maps, success often followed. Without the maps, everyone journeyed into a world unfamiliar to them.

Today, in our own lives, each of us has a journey to fulfill. Sometimes it is also into unknown territory. Often we have neither understanding nor maps.

And, sometimes, we are lost.

So, how do you get from the world of yesterday, a world of past reality, into the world of today and tomorrow? How do you begin to transform yourself?

How do you leave behind an unworkable life, even though that life might be filled with events and feelings you don't want anymore...feelings such as anxiety, fear, anger, loneliness, or resentment?

How do you exit the struggle and the pain without succumbing to suicide or fatal illness?

How do you do it? How do you make the map? Where can you find the answers? Who can you turn to in your vulnerability?

In my case, over the past ten years, if not my entire lifetime, this journey from then to now has taken me on a road through a place called *Lost*. By some, "Lost" may be interpreted as a metaphor. For me, this place called Lost is real.

I have been traveling through Lost a number of years. I have met others along the way who have also come to realize that *Lost is a place, too.*

Perhaps one day you will find yourself face-to-face with an unfamiliar crossroad, disoriented, in pain, feeling deep despair and aware that what you thought you knew about yourself, what you assumed about the world, is not true, that those assumptions are no longer correct. This realization shatters everyday life into pieces of fear.

The next step is crucial. Perverse, even ludicrous, the next moments are, literally, opportunities of this lifetime.

These moments may last just a few hours or they may happen over many years. They are the moments of transformation, those magical moments of change and growth. Ironically, they often occur just as we find ourselves entering a place called Lost.

My life has been filled with these crucial moments for the majority of the past ten years. Some moments I recognized as they were occurring, others I understood only in hindsight.

In looking back it is clear to me that these series of transition moments were grouped in several different categories, although ultimately connected to one another and built on each other's shared experiences.

The first major change took me from thinking of myself as the victimized child, through being an adult victim and into becoming a survivor. I had to move through all the various stages fully.

Next came opportunities for learning kindness toward myself and the process of creating a nurturing environment in which to live my life. These have been difficult lessons because my childhood gave me neither role models nor adequate life skills by which to guide my adult course. Too often, when we think about being kind to ourselves, we think in terms of simply feeding our familiar addictions. It takes time and patience to figure out what behavior is truly satisfying and beneficial rather than just temporarily reducing the feelings of pain and emptiness.

The third portion of this triangular transformative process is an ongoing one, centered on making connections between my life and the powers that create safety in the universe. This transformation could only have happened by facing my ultimate fear, which was of death itself.

My spiritual umbilical cord had been severed in illness and needed to be reconstructed but I could not accomplish that task until the value of life was made my primary focus.

From there, everything else would flow and I would find my true connection with the universe as a safe haven of spiritual growth and nurturance.

It is a long journey to take in one short lifetime. And many were the years I have wandered through the place called Lost, befriended only by my own dreams and illusions of the phantasma.

So, as you have come across this book, perhaps it is because you are wandering through Lost. Perhaps this book will provide a map for you. Perhaps these pages, the story of my journey, will nurture you and, in time, you will see the validation of your own experience.

Of course the map will not tell you how the sky looks in the morning, nor how the air around you smells, nor how an outstretched hand feels, nor how some eyes share the secrets of their soul with another, nor what life is.

It is just a map. You choose which path to take, which course to chart, even if you don't know exactly where you're going. It is you who experience.

Some call this process sheer foolishness. I have learned to call it absolute faith and the ability to follow your inner voice.

Whatever you want it to be... it is.

I share these moments with you in the knowledge that you will make of them what is appropriate for you. You will take what you need and leave the remainder.

So, with a sense of love surrounding all of us, I place before you the journey as it happened.

PART ONE

PHANTASMA

TRUTH—
THE CATALYST

THERE IS ABOUT the truth an atmosphere of excitement, a pervasive public interest that is not created by publicity and will not subside when the press leaves. It is a groundswell that touches every corner of ordinary life. The truth is also controversial. It creates heated arguments. It tests people's belief systems. Sometimes it temporarily polarizes factions of society.

The truth is exposé; a fundamental reexamination of something that has been taken for granted over a long period of time. Suddenly, people face-to-face with truth look at life with a different perspective. Things that were formally hidden now become glaringly apparent.

Truth is a point of demarcation. As with a major national event or disaster, human emotions are forced to the surface to combat the probability of uncertainty and even chaos.

Over the long run, truth is a catalyst. Though the understanding of truth may come as a lightning flash, the full realization of it over time changes many elements in the intricate fabric of our lives and connects events that previously seemed unrelated.

My truth became a book, an autobiography titled *Mommie Dearest*.

It is hard to remember that there was a time when the word "dearest" after someone's name didn't carry a negative double meaning, when ordinary hangers made of wire were not synonymous with anything other than the dry cleaners, when the connotation of the term "Mommie Dearest" had not been incorporated into everyday American language, and when child abuse was a hidden family tragedy not discussed in public, not recognized as a national issue. But that was before my book was published early in November 1978.

Looking back to early summer, 1977, when I began writing *Mommie Dearest*, Los Angeles was already in the midst of a severe drought. Temperatures over 105 degrees every day were no longer unusual. Water was rationed through meter reading and stiff penalties were imposed on violators.

The front yard at our small house on Beckford Avenue was brown. The lawn died in June. The asphalt driveway was dusty. We had two window air conditioners. One was in the bedroom and the other in the living room, but they both faded by mid-afternoon when the wind-driven Santa Ana heat blasted across the San Fernando Valley.

Every day I sat in the living room typing page after page on my old gray Royal standard. I aimed for ten pages a day, but sometimes the output was twenty or more. The days of past and present fused into one another as I delved further and further into those terrifying years. Entire memories suddenly appeared unannounced, jolting me into insights I hadn't anticipated.

Many, many days there were tears streaming down my face for hours. I lost count of the times I cried. It didn't matter. What surprised me was only that I thought I had cried those tears before. I thought that they had ended with the past.

As the days proceeded, so did the number of pages. So did my personal journey into a tangled nightmare from which I'd never completely recovered. Early in the pages I decided to recollect how it felt as a *child* experiencing the confusion, the lack of information, the events which seemed to have no beginning and no end, but just to have a middle in which I was eternally caught. I concentrated on remembering the feelings when someone important to my life disappeared. It shocked me to realize that as a child, I had lost almost everyone I loved.

Slowly most of the pieces of my life went together even when I still didn't understand why or how. That dual sense of discovery and helplessness was the very element that I was trying to elicit in the pages of my writing.

It was a painful process. It made me feel little and vulnerable. I wanted to hide. There were many days when I felt as though I had no skin to cover me. Those were very new and scary days. I felt too vulnerable to leave the safety of my home even to venture out to the supermarket.

Magically, I had been transported into the past. The past hurt. I was often immobilized by reliving the shame and sense of worthlessness I had experienced as a child. Once again I saw the night terrors and felt the choking hands, the clawing cold. As through a mysterious two-way mirror, I witnessed the few rays of hope sparkle and grow only to be dashed by ridicule or punishment.

I felt a renewed sense of frustration and anger about the raw injustice and incompetence which had surrounded my early life. As I wrote, it became clear that when I was a child there was no way out for me. I was locked into the struggle.

What I had been forced to learn about life was only the struggle, never the reward. All I knew was a gut reaction to survive.

What emerged was an awful truth: the battle of my relationship with my mother was forever, because *it was still inside me.* But even before the publication of my book I realized as an adult that in order to save my own life and my soul, I had to leave her—and find myself. That process almost killed me.

CHAOS

IN SAN LUIS OBISPO, California, it was August 2, 1981.

This Sunday morning was going to be hot. At nine o'clock the temperature was already nearing eighty-five degrees when my husband and I reached the riding instructor's small farm. I was excited by the progress of my riding lessons. David watched outside the corral, awaiting his turn.

We were both trying to find ways of stepping out of the whirlwind of the book's publicity tours, of preparing for the release of the film *Mommie Dearest*—and getting back to life as we had understood it. And, in order to bring some humanity back into our marriage instead of just maintaining it as a business partnership between two workaholics, we were also trying to make room for entertainment and fun. We had decided that one way of achieving this goal would be the shared experience of riding lessons.

Our instructor, Janice, coached my moves in concert with the horse. It was one of those rare moments when everything timed out right—the animal and rider in synchronized communication. We went from trot to canter on command. As the bay gelding surged forward, I felt a rush of freedom, of perfection. The warm sun bathed my face with tiny pin-pricks of perspiration. I felt my long blond hair begin to stick to the back of my neck. As I turned the far corner of the riding ring, I glanced directly at my husband. I realized I must be grinning like a kid yelling "look at me" because that is how he smiled happily back as we passed.

I wanted this morning to last forever. My childhood fantasy was coming true. In just a few more weeks David and I were going to be able to ride horseback together on our ranch, free as two birds, exploring the hidden trails and the wilderness in confidence.

With the pride normally attributed to a parent watching her kids winning a competition, I traded places and watched my husband complete his lesson. We'd been through so much together, worked so hard—it was wonderful to see him enjoying himself.

As I stood beside this wooden corral dressed in my jeans and boots it was a mark of progress for me to quietly remember how very different life had been in the past.

From 1958 until 1972 I was an actress in theater and television. But even before starting my own acting career, I had been a celebrity all my life, growing up in the camera lens of my mother's studio publicity photos. Being on display was not foreign to me nor did it seem special. It had been so much a part of my world from the very beginning as Joan Crawford's adopted daughter that it was just a given factor in life's equation of stardom and the power of money.

In a world where money is not just a single value, but often the only value, the money itself takes on human characteristics.

Clean or dirty, productive or unproductive, new or old, gross or class. These anthropomorphized money terms denoting personal traits are qualities we also apply to ourselves as human beings.

It is harder still to separate money from our feelings with regard to it. Loss of money equals grief, gain of money equals happiness, management of money equals mixed feelings of being trapped by it or not wanting to be responsible for it. Making money is fantasized as bringing success. "More is better"—but often equals only compulsive behavior loaded with high stress.

When money is the only value, we do things, behave in a way never imagined in other circumstances.

If you have money—or are perceived by others to have money—it appears that you are not entitled to have any serious problems. Or if you persist in having problems, you are not entitled to compassion from others, because the value of having money should compensate you well enough and provide you with adequate means of solving the difficulty.

Before *Mommie Dearest* was published, I was still caught up in that thought pattern about money.

Since childhood, my life revolved around what money could do, what money could buy, who could be influenced, and how money could bend the rules by which people without money were supposed to live, if not suspend those rules entirely.

I learned about the personalities of the men and women who could be bought, saw the power and sexual attraction of not just the money itself, but the ensuing power that money people assumed as an inherent right.

Money, the amount of it and the power surrounding it, was the social order, the driving force through which my young world operated. I was taught the rigid rules of gentility: how to eat properly, how to speak correctly, how to smile appropriately, when to exit, when, even, to flirt. Somewhere between princess and courtesan, my training progressed until it became evident that this training was not just for my benefit. I, too, had been bought with the power of money. My life was an adjunct, an amenity, a human prop in a much larger performance.

When that realization became intolerable for me to live with, I left home, with nothing to guide me except this elaborate training appropriate only to the world of money and power.

I had never felt safe in my whole life. I had never known whom to trust. I had never known what it was like to feel cared for or nurtured. And whenever I had cried, I had cried by myself, alone. I never remember being held gently in loving arms while I was in tears or trying to work out a problem either as a child or as a young adult.

My childhood home was not a safe place. Not even my own bedroom had been safe. Adults were not safe—they dealt in treachery. Friends were not safe—they could not keep secrets.

On my own, finding myself on the streets of New York City, armed only with eighteen years of life experience, it is a miracle I survived at all. None of my skills were geared toward making money and since there was no provision for either income or trust fund from my family, it was crucial for me to learn rapidly how to earn a living.

But, even at the depth of my personal despair and in the midst of very real fears about becoming a teenage bag lady, I carried with me some of the instincts of breeding that were undeniable. Sometimes it worked against me; I'd look for work only to be confronted with lots of questions about being a movie star's daughter. I'd ask for help and not be believed. Sometimes other people thought I must be "slumming"—a term used in the late fifties indicating the behavior of upper-class people who wanted to see what "real" life was like and traveled to Harlem to hear jazz music and Greenwich Village for coffee and poetry with the beatniks.

I, however, was actually living among the jazz musicians, the numbers runners, drunks in tenement hallways and acute poverty.

My mother rode in black limousines and lived in a penthouse on Fifth Avenue, less than ten blocks away. I collected neighborhood beer bottles, turning them in for the nickel refund in order to pay the fifteen-cent bus fare each day and buy cigarettes.

Life inevitably got better for me, but it was a slow and painful lesson. However, that act of sheer survival became the basis of my tenuous self-esteem.

There were so many things I didn't know how to ask questions about. So many things about the world that were not a part of my experience.

My knowledge contained a bizarre mixture of life at the very top and survival at the very bottom—nothing in between—nothing ordinary, nothing immediately useful.

Southern California, Laurel Canyon, in the early sixties was a little safer. I guess I was a hippie long before the media coined such a name for the emergence of a counterculture based on ideas of community instead of separateness. Almost everyone grew marijuana on the hillsides of Laurel Canyon. Most people planted it camouflaged in the middle of tomato bushes, which apparently worked well because no one ever seemed to get caught. And, "grass" was the drug of choice. Unlike New York, there weren't as many hard drugs, street drugs, killer drugs until LSD came around. The original movement grew out of economic dis-enfranchisement. We were thrown together, black and white, male and female, because the establishment locked us out of jobs, out of power, out of the money mainstream. The drug culture and Viet Nam came later, six or eight years later. In the beginning we were poor, discontented and invisible. It was later that we were radical and marched publicly in the streets.

So, for the ten years between 1960 and 1970 I wandered back and forth across this country. LA/NY–NY/LA like a migrant worker—an actress, a gypsy, a lost soul; looking for work, looking for love, searching for a place to belong, maybe someday even finding a sense of safety.

Along the way, a lot of people passed by me. With some I tried work, with others friendship. One of my fellow travelers even tried a brief two-year marriage with me.

Deep inside there was a part of me that remained closed despite the laughter, the progress, the earning of money, the accomplishments of my life. Out of a childhood of isolation and terror I had built an adult life of competence and responsibility.

The sadness I felt about all of my success was just a dominant color that permeated my life; There was not a real feeling about it. I was not yet in touch with the terror that motivated me.

I couldn't possibly face the sadness yet. I was still too angry about the past and too scared about the future to recognize my own grief, my sadness or loss.

And so, I relied heavily on my competence and sense of responsibility, on my ability to "take care" of things, people, family. I knew how to shoulder burdens. I knew how to work. I knew how to tolerate pain. I had to survive and endure. I drew people to me through instinctively guessing what they needed and then providing it for them, as though I were feeding their addiction.

I was driven to survive to get closer to where I had been, to succeed so that the suffocating sense of loss, humiliation, grief about the present course of my life would subside. It was not all right with me. I was scared every moment during my years out on the streets, longing to be protected and cared about, to feel secure and special. But there was no one to ask and no one from whom to receive. So I decided against needing, against caring, against trusting, against being nurtured and went forward with the business of survival.

When my efforts to make money through my acting career began to succeed, my desire was always to hold onto it for dear life. It was the one source of comfort, of safety, of peace and warmth. I hadn't yet learned about the value of money as a means of freedom. All I knew about money was in terms of right now, in terms of primitive security. I could breathe when there was money. My eyes could see, ears could hear. Without it, all systems shut down to concentrate only on survival.

Money sends out vibrations like blood attracting sharks. Substantial amounts of money spark the people-sharks into a feeding frenzy, exhibiting characteristics of sexual excitement, greed and pure treachery.

David and I first met in Los Angeles in 1971 when he was a commercial producer for a large Detroit advertising agency and I was still an actress.

Late one afternoon I got an urgent call to audition for a Chevrolet commercial, but only if I could be at the studio in half an hour. It was the fall season and I was hunting for antique furniture, specifically a dining room table, to complete my spacious 1920's-era Hollywood Hills apartment.

There was no time to wash my long blond hair or even take a shower. So I put on a little makeup, wrapped a scarf around my hair, changed jeans and shirt and dashed out the door.

David and the director were sitting behind a table facing me in the audition room. They both looked exhausted. David wore dark glasses but I saw deep shadows under his eyes. Since there were only two lines of dialogue to read, I was puzzled as to why they were having difficulty casting.

The director began to explain the commercial. He said it was a *truck* job and they had interviewed every female *stunt driver* in town!

"What kind of truck?" I asked, trying to sound nonchalant while envisioning myself trying to learn to drive an 18-wheeler in two days. Actors never say no to a great job.

"The biggest pick-up Chevy makes, with the biggest camper it will carry," the director replied.

My relief must have been obvious because we both smiled.

"I just did a pick-up truck test last month," I told him, rather delighted with myself.

"That's why you're here," he said flatly. David evaluated me silently.

"Well, that sounds like great fun," I chattered on. "Years ago I had friends who were into sports car racing and they taught me all the basics. Even let me do the warm-up laps. I'm a California girl. I grew up loving cars and speed."

Technically, I was not a stunt driver, but I could certainly drive well enough for this job since the sponsor wanted a woman who would photograph like the All-American housewife on vacation with husband and kids.

As I walked back into my apartment, the phone was ringing. The agent told me I got the truck commercial. Several days later I went to work for the man who was to be my second husband. For years David delighted in telling everyone that he'd met me when I was a stunt driver on a truck shoot! Indeed, the expressions on people's faces were priceless to behold. It was such a macho introduction in stark contrast to whatever their fantasy had about me been.

After 1972, when I made the decision to leave show business, finish college, and seek a corporate job, I no longer sought the celebrity limelight as a way to earn a living. In fact, it was my intention never to be in front of the camera again. After so many years, it was a relief not to have to wear as much makeup, to be able to wear less flashy clothes and make an impression with my intelligence instead of my appearance.

David, was freelancing as a commercial producer and in 1975, after I completed graduate school at USC with a master's degree in Communication Management, I worked for Getty Oil in their Corporate Public Relations Department at a modest salary.

On our income after we were married in 1976, we owned two used cars and a modest, two-bedroom house with a small pool in Tarzana, California. David's son, who lived with us, attended a local public junior high school.

Our life was a busy, happy, middle-class Southern California existence.

As I stood by the horse corral this summer morning in 1981, I realized that my career over the past three years had skyrocketed. I had written two books, three major national magazine articles, several screenplay drafts (for the film) and had appeared on hundreds, maybe even thousands of radio or television talk shows, as well as having been on-camera narrator for a documentary film called *Victims*. In fact it often amused me to think that I'd probably spent more time in *front* of the camera in these last three years than I had during my previous acting career! Now the *Mommie Dearest* publicity tours were over. I had finished the final draft of my second book, a novel titled *Black Widow*, and the Paramount Picture film version of *Mommie Dearest* was complete. The film would be released in the fall and *Black Widow* was scheduled for winter publication.

It amazed me that nearly everyone still seemed to have a very strong opinion both about the book, *Mommie Dearest*, and the person, Christina Crawford.

However, I often wondered if such a person existed at all. What I saw printed about me, the opinions people seemed to have of the book—both positive and negative—were very far removed from my perception either of myself or my work.

During the heat of this controversy, a strange thing began to occur. As I started to be recognized wherever I went, I could feel myself beginning to withdraw. I didn't want to go anywhere if there were crowds. I just wanted to stay home, unless I absolutely had to appear for work. I particularly did not want to be in airports.

The one place to which I did enjoy going was our ranch in San Luis Obispo, which was about a three-hour drive north of Los Angeles. So, when David finished work as executive producer on the Paramount film, we made weekly trips north.

All the way back to the ranch that Sunday morning we talked about what kinds of horses to get, when we should start looking, and how much fun we were going to have. We were like two children the day before Christmas.

After lunch in Morro Bay, overlooking the water, we drove back to Los Angeles, preparing to meet another busy week. It was so rare for either of us to be able to spend much time anymore just having fun.

In Tarzana, California, it was Monday, August 3, 1981.

At seven-thirty in the morning I left for my exercise class. The gym was only a ten-minute drive from my house and the first session was never crowded. After the class and my routine with the weights, I took a leisurely sauna and shower. I could still feel a slight tenderness in my leg muscles from the previous day's riding lesson, but the sauna helped.

When I returned home at about nine, my mother-in-law was having coffee. Dorothy and I sat at the kitchen table laughing and talking as we did most mornings during her summer visit from Detroit. As I got up to put my cup in the dishwasher, she asked me a question.

For a moment I sensed something was strange. I had trouble managing the dishwasher door and couldn't seem to understand what she'd asked me. I stared at Dorothy, embarrassed to admit I hadn't paid attention. Suddenly my mind seemed to go blank. There were no words. It was an awkward situation, entirely unlike my usual behavior. Finally, I managed to tell her I was going to change clothes and left the kitchen abruptly.

Alone in my bathroom, I studied my face in the large mirror. Nothing about me looked as peculiar as I felt. I proceeded to take a shower, wash my hair, put on a little makeup and get dressed in a peach shirt and a brightly flowered cotton skirt.

David was on the phone in our office/guest house by the time I was ready to work. There was a stack of papers I needed to read pertaining to the child-abuse-prevention charity of which I was currently president.

I sat down on the couch in the office waiting for David to finish his conversation and started to read the first page of the lengthy report. Suddenly the entire sheaf of papers fell out of my hands. I felt faint. Carefully, and with some difficulty, I gathered up the papers. I sat silently, wondering what was going on. Taking a deep breath to calm myself, I started reading once again. The whole stack of papers slipped out of my right hand and fell on the floor for a second time.

Something was wrong with me. Without saying anything, I left the office went to my bedroom in the house and lay down.

Something very strange was affecting both my body and my mind, but I didn't know what it was. My right hand didn't seem to be functioning properly. It was now shaking as though a nerve in my arm or shoulder had been pinched, causing the hand to convulse. A few minutes before, it had fallen limp.

I tried to think logically and calmly about what I should do, but my mind also seemed to be playing tricks on me. One minute I could reason with words that were normal and the next minute nothing came out right, nothing made sense. I was beginning to feel a nauseating sensation of panic come over me.

I went to the bedroom door and called across the back yard for my husband.

David hurried into the room and looked at me lying on the bed. I saw fear register on his face.

"What's the matter?" he asked gently, trying to guess the problem by himself.

"My hand...doesn't work...and I can't talk right."

He called for his mother, who was a nurse. Dorothy took my blood pressure and pulse, checking for signs of a heart attack. David called the paramedics. He and Dorothy covered me with a blanket.

The paramedics arrived in less than ten minutes. Our two dogs barked incessantly, quite beside themselves at the sight of uniformed men entering the house. There was a general state of confusion.

It was difficult for me to explain what was wrong. I didn't have any pain; there was no place where it hurt. My speech was better than a few minutes before and the feeling was back in my right hand.

At first the paramedic said he thought I was suffering from hyperventilation. To my somewhat confused mind his words translated as "hypochondria!" How I wished it were all a bad dream, a figment of imagination; for if it was a bad dream, it would all be over soon and I could go back to work.

However, at the same time the paramedic was explaining hyperventilation to David, my right hand and arm went into a convulsion.

Everyone stared silently at me.

"I want to go to the hospital." My voice sounded like the pleading of a small child.

There was little further discussion. The paramedics lifted me onto the gurney and into the waiting ambulance. David was to follow in his car. The two dogs now went quite berserk seeing two uniformed strangers carting me away on a stretcher. The noise level and anxiety were making everything seem unreal to me.

The hospital was only a mile away. The paramedics wheeled me into the emergency room, where the nurse and staff doctor took over. My right hand was numb. I was having trouble speaking.

When the doctor asked me to describe my condition, I

said, "I can't *hear* my right hand." What I had meant to say was that I couldn't *feel* the hand. The nurse said I had "aphasic" speech patterns. Vaguely I recalled that aphasia was related to brain damage. The feeling of panic over-whelmed me again. I started to cry. Tears streamed down my face.

David's face suddenly appeared around the curtain. I clung to his hand, tears still streaming down my face. "I want to get dressed and go home." I wanted to pretend that nothing terrible was happening to me.

"They've located a neurologist, honey, and the doctor will be in to see you very soon," he told me. It was not yet noon.

As I lay helplessly in the emergency room, the attacks seemed to get closer in their cyclic occurrences. Now, as my right arm lost control and thrashed, my speech slurred or the wrong words came out.

My mind whirled. I couldn't control my thoughts. Then the whirling mind would stop and return me to a normal state for a short time.

I was scared to death. David was trying to comfort me, cradling me in his arms, talking softly to me.

"It is going to be all right...it is going to be all right... honest, baby, it's going to be all right." Then he was gone and in his place stood a nurse.

The nurse came over, removed my shoes, my gold chain necklace and earrings, taking all jewelry except my wedding band, which I held onto.

When he finally arrived, the young neurologist was pleas-ant and spoke softly. The more he talked, the faster I felt myself drifting into unreality. I was very frightened and confused—so confused, in fact, that I was only able to piece together the entire story from details related by David, the doctors, nurses and my friends.

At this point David had been sent to the waiting room, where he paced, leaving only occasionally to have a cigarette outside.

"Mr. Koontz," the doctor called, summoning him. "The first test is going to be a spinal tap. You will need to sign a release consent form."

"Sixteen years ago my son had that same test and the thought scares the hell out of me. I'll never forget the scream that came from that two-year-old boy's throat when they put that needle in his back," David said to the doctor. Then he added, "God, that's going to hurt her. Please don't hurt her."

The doctor replied, "It won't, I promise you."

Reluctantly, David signed the form, and waited, alone once more. Another eternity was passing...the time between reports seemed to be so long. Finally, the doctor came out.

"What is it? What's the matter with her?"

The neurologist answered, "I can't tell now. We'll wait a little bit. The tests should be back in another twenty minutes, but it seems as though she's stroking out."

The word *stroke* hit David like a brick. Stroking... stroking..."God, are you telling me that she's having a stroke?"

He said, "We have to get these tests to find out if there's any blood in her spinal column."

"Can I see her?"

"Yes, you can see her. Go on back, she's all right," the doctor replied.

"David, I don't know what's the matter with me."

"Sweetheart. They're going to check..."

"What did the doctor tell you?"

"He wouldn't tell me anything—only that they had to wait

for the tests to come through, but they are going to admit you to the hospital for tests that may last three or four days."

"David, I don't want to die. What's wrong with me?"

"I don't know, sweetheart, I don't know, but they'll find out."

Two orderlies arrived, wrapped the sheet tightly around me, transferred me to a gurney bed and transported me to a fourth-floor semi-private room, where nurses tried to make me comfortable.

Beautiful flowers arrived. I was surprised that anyone knew I was in the hospital.

I stared at the large arrangement of luscious deep pink roses. The fragrance from them filled the room, temporarily masking the pervasive hospital smell. I glanced at my right arm, which was lying on top of the sheet, motionless. I felt my mind quietly sinking into a strange world previously unknown to me.

Life sensations of my mind and body were ebbing away from me. My thoughts and feelings became muted in this foreign land where any ability to communicate with the world outside my own being was impossible.

The solitary link between me and other people was my husband, David. I dimly realized that my illness was isolating me, dwindling all my faculties to near zero. My right side was paralyzed. I couldn't talk. I couldn't think.

By the time David returned from the Admissions office, the doctor was there. "There is no blood in her spinal column, in the spinal fluid, but another test is required."

The next test was a CAT scan. "What is that?" David asked when they told him to sign another form.

Tarzana Medical Center was testing the new CAT scanner, the latest in the technological development of that method of sophisticated X ray technique. It was located in a separate mobile unit.

The large ramp was lowered and the orderlies put the stretcher on the ramp, which rose as would an elevator, and I was wheeled into this 21st-century–looking device. Carefully they transferred me to a table that would move in micro inches to position me where my entire brain would be scanned.

CAT scan—the space age. For me it was like being inside a space capsule during launch. The inner noise was incredible. I was terrified. I tried to pray.

Please God . . . help me . . . help me . . . help me not to die like this.

The two words—God and help—are all I thought. The noise and mirror white, clear brightness are intolerable. The sound is deafening. The sound and brightness pierce themselves into my brain. I am overwhelmed with terror. No movement. "DON'T MOVE," they say. The time is forever now God . . . help . . . Everything is now totally out of my control—my mind, my body, my life. I can't stand it.

Later, the doctor came back into the hospital room to announce that there was nothing wrong inside the brain. They couldn't find any blood clot or anything. He could not understand why I was continually "stroking out." He had spoken with our family doctor and the two of them agreed on a medication, Heparin, which they immediately administered.

Less than an hour later, two friends arrived and took David down the street to a local restaurant. David told them about the fact that the doctors had mentioned the word *stroke*. No one could believe it. One friend said, "David, Christina is simply too young and too healthy to have a stroke."

* * *

David was a wreck, trying to hold it together, trying to be calm, trying to explain in detail to me and our friends everything that had been said and done. On the walk back to the hospital he broke down and cried.

That night the doctor came back, announcing that the tests were all negative—they showed absolutely nothing wrong. But he looked worried, as though he didn't know what to do now.

At that point David got a pad of paper and a pencil and tried to help write out what I was trying to say. He wrote the letters of the alphabet and asked me to point to the one relating to a word. I couldn't do it. As David sat with me that night, trying to calm me down, every now and then a tear would roll down my cheek, but I knew that I couldn't communicate.

Occasionally David would talk with me. Slowly, as the night hours continued, he prayed. "Dear God, please help Christina, please help my wife, please help your angel... she's worked so hard on your behalf. Please spare her, allow her to come back. Please I beg you, dear God."

What he did not know was that the worst was yet to come. He thought he had bottomed out. He thought he had reached the time where it couldn't be any worse.

At eleven o'clock, Monday night, David saw me slip into a comalike state.

David called the nurse, then got the doctor on the phone. "Do something, do something, you can't just let my wife slip away in the middle of the night!"

As the next day wore on, David began to get angry. Everyone knew his wife was having a stroke, but none of the doctors knew what was causing it. *Why didn't they?* He raged inwardly. Why couldn't they pull together all of the information to be able to say what was going on and to help make Christina well?

Even though many people came to visit on Tuesday, I was in no condition to see anybody. It was very, very difficult because I kept slipping in and out of the comalike state. So, a lot of friends spent the time trying to comfort David, who kept saying "I'm all right. She's the one who has the problem. Please pray for her."

The decision was finally made that they would do an angiogram Wednesday morning. The angiogram is an internal X ray of the vascular system in the entire body. The doctors were clear about the enormous risk to my life in performing this test, but this was the last major test they would be able to do.

The number of flowers I had received was absolutely overwhelming. At one point a friend jokingly complained that she didn't think she was going to be able to breathe because the flowers were taking all the oxygen.

It was into this veritable garden that Dr. Roland Summit came at ten on Wednesday morning. David had called him earlier at my request. We knew each other from several years of child-abuse-prevention work.

About eleven o'clock, our visit was interrupted. A nonintrusive machine was hooked up to me, much like the multiple hookup of an electrocardiogram, only this test was to allow them literally to see my heart on a small television. My heart was perfectly normal. That was the maddening thing. Every single test had come out completely normal. The doctors were stumped totally.

After the test, Dr. Summit sat quietly with David and me. As both friend and psychiatrist, he talked with us about the whole process of dying. He saw it was obvious that I thought

I was going to die soon. He also understood my feelings of being punished once again as though I were back in childhood. He was trying to talk me through that, trying to bolster my spirits and get me to fight for life and not give up.

I cried a lot and could talk very little. More flowers kept arriving.

At one o'clock they began the angiogram test.

The room temperature and the steel table feel very cold on my bare skin. The dye they inject into my leg burns red hot, searing through every part of my body. The angiogram is excruciating pain. The doctor has said, "The most dangerous of the tests. Through an artery in the groin dye is injected. X rays then photograph any blockages." The pain is beyond comprehension. If I am to die, why must I be tortured? Why can't I die with the flowers in my room, holding David's hand? This is barbaric. The pain is unbelievable. God help me.

The big X ray–viewing room was intended to be for the absolutely private use of the medical staff. However, the doctors soon found it was useless to ask David or Dr. Summit to leave. The X rays of my vascular system were developed and posted on wall racks.

Finally, they could see the cause. There was an embolism, a blockage in the left carotid artery leading up to the base of the brain. The X ray was crystal clear. The embolism was about three and a half inches long, located less than one-eighth of an inch away from the base of the brain, and extended downward the length of the artery.

The neurologist was visibly horrified when he found the embolism on the X ray. He looked at it and he said he didn't know what to do. As far as he was concerned, it was totally inoperable, but he was to consult with a vascular surgeon and a neurosurgeon.

The only man in Los Angeles who could perform such complex, experimental surgery was Dr. Milton Heifetz at Cedars Sinai Hospital.

After a few frantic phone calls the operation was scheduled for that same afternoon. Heifetz was going to do a new procedure called an intracranial bypass. David almost fainted. On one hand he was elated that they had found the problem, on the other hand he was now terrified. Roland Summit never left. He stayed with David, explaining medical terminology and being supportive as the terrible strain increased.

The doctors immediately stopped the Heparin, concerned that the medication might kick loose a part of the huge clot in the carotid artery.

I requested that all my flowers be given to the children in this hospital, since I understood I was being transferred to Cedars Sinai.

Five o'clock rolled around and still there was no ambulance. David went to the nurses' station and begged one of the nurses to check and see what had happened to the ambulance. He was frustrated and angry.

Meanwhile, Drs. Heifetz and Weingarten were standing by at Cedars Sinai waiting for my arrival. The nurse called and spoke with Dr. Heifetz. He said, "Get her here. Don't you understand that with every minute that goes by her life is further threatened?" At five-thirty David found out that the first ambulance had broken down! He called the Los Angeles paramedics who arrived within twenty minutes.

I am in a police ambulance going to Cedars Sinai, Hospital, eighteen miles away. A woman paramedic holds my head steady the entire trip. I am to be operated on by a neurosurgeon. Please, God, let him help me.

On arrival, they took me into the intensive care unit at Cedars Sinai to prepare me quickly for the operation.

"Wait a minute," David called. "I haven't talked to the doctor...I have to talk to him...what's going on here? What's going to happen? What kind of operation is going to be performed?"

The nurse said, "You mean you haven't been told? Hold on just one second." She went running out to get the doctor.

Dr. Heifetz came in immediately. He said, "Come with me, although I must tell you we don't have much time." They went into a small room.

He very carefully explained that he was going to do an intracranial bypass because there was no possible chance of helping me by operating on the carotid artery. It was, in fact, inoperable.

"What are her chances?"

He said, "My young man, very slim."

He explained that what he was going to do was open the skull and go into the brain and bring over an artery from the right side under the tissue and into the brain, thereby bypassing the normal blood flow.

"What would you do if this were your wife?"

"I would operate."

"If we didn't operate, what would happen?"

He said, "I can't tell you that. She might make it, but if she were mine, I would operate."

Dr. Heifetz is staring down at me. I feel him touch me. I sense that he has very strong hands and penetrating dark eyes. He explains the procedure. I nod yes; I look at David who has always been with me. I can't talk, but with my eyes I try to tell my husband that I love him. My one thought as they wheel me into the operating room is:

I never thought it would end like this. Please God, don't let me die.

"Let's go. Get her in there," Heifetz ordered.

Off they went, out through the big stainless-steel-covered door across the hall and straight toward the pre-op room, which was, in fact, a "clean" room. David, in his street clothes, walked right into the room where they were wheeling me.

"Stop, stop!" All kinds of nurses and doctors were shouting at him.

"You can't be in here in street clothes. Get out of here."

"But I haven't had a chance to say good-bye to my...I haven't had a chance to say good-bye to her...wait, please."

They pushed David out of the room, but they immediately brought him an operating gown, a hat, booties and a mask.

"Okay, come with us," a nurse said, motioning.

"Christina, I love you, sweetheart. Everything is going to be okay. I'll be right here. Just pray to God. Yes, baby, it'll be okay. I'll see you in a little while..." he kissed me.

I smiled, and tears formed in my eyes. They wheeled me off.

Near midnight, Dr. Heifetz and Dr. Weingarten came out into the waiting room dressed in their street clothes, with very stern, somber looks on their faces.

Dr. Heifetz came over and sat down.

"Mr. Koontz, I want to talk to you..."

"Is she all right?"

He said, "I must explain to you, when I opened her up, she was too far gone…"

David was speechless.

Dr. Heifetz said, "I had no idea there had been such massive damage done. When I opened her up, I saw she was too far gone. I could not do the operation."

He continued. "David, if I had touched the membrane containing her brain…she was too hot, her brain was too hot…it was too damaged. If I had touched the membrane, her brain would have squirted out on the floor."

He said, "I did a temporary fix and patched her back up. Believe me, Mr. Koontz, there is nothing more that can be done for your wife. What I did may work, and may not. I will tell you that she has maybe a one percent chance."

"Of living? Is she going to die?"

He said, "No…worse…She has a one percent chance of not being a total vegetable all her life…It might be a blessing if it doesn't work, if she does die."

He continued slowly. "I never imagined that she was this bad. The only thing that can help is to pray to God…"

David thought his mother was going to have a heart attack, because even though his attention never faltered for one second from Dr. Heifetz' face and mouth, David heard his mother scream.

Heifetz had finished saying, "It's minute by minute. If she makes it one minute, then she has another minute, and if she makes it through the first five minutes, then she has another five minutes."

Then Dr. Heifetz got up, put his hand on David's shoulder, and left. David sat in a trance, the words burning into his brain, burning into his soul and his heart like molten lava.

"Please God, don't let her die, don't let her die."

* * *

SURVIVOR

Sounds and some faint sensation reach through. My body is a lead weight. It is very cold. I don't yet know whether I am dead, in purgatory, or alive in the hospital. How had I gotten here?

I have the feeling that I am journeying to another realm. I see a place with brilliant darkness alive with millions of lights like stars. It is a bright blue space. I see myself like a spirit surrounded by and yet inside the starlight's brightness. I wasn't exactly a part of the stars and didn't have their shape but I was among them and a part of their light. It is beautiful blue space, clear but not like the sky or like water either.

I feel myself falling and floating through this space. It is not like anything I've ever seen in movies or known in my dreams before. This is a special place. A place of vastness and of peace. A blue space punctuated by crystal clear brightness. Perhaps now I am going now to visit all my hopes and dreams, the same ones I sent skyward during the years of my childhood. Perhaps I will be able to see my beloved stars at close range. Maybe this is the conclusion to the dream itself, the dream that started almost forty years ago.

Then abruptly, something or someone catches my fall. It seems to me that I am held for a moment in the hands of the Universe. I am traveling through the blue space on the wings of prayer. Am I going back to earth or continuing through in this realm of blue and crystal stars?

How had it all come to this?

MOMMIE DEAREST

THE SAME MONTH my mother died, May 1977, I left my corporate job of two years and started a dispute with the unemployment office over whether or not I was to be awarded compensation. Every two weeks I stood in line while they reviewed my case and sent me home without any money.

In June I caught pneumonia. We didn't have health insurance since David was freelancing and I was unemployed so I hoped I could get well without going to a hospital. As I rested outside in the shade I had plenty of time to think. Two or three weeks later I got up and started writing the book that became *Mommie Dearest*. My life was never the same again.

A few months after I started writing, David and I had dinner with Bernie and Mildred Berkowitz, my former therapists from New York and authors of the bestseller, *How to Be Your Own Best Friend*. I asked Bernie if he'd read some pages of my book and let me know what he thought. A couple of weeks later we spoke again and he offered to give the twenty pages to his agent in New York.

To my surprise, the agent called within a few days. She told me she was interested in seeing more when she returned from her vacation after Labor Day weekend.

September 1977: the typing was finished. It had been a tough summer. The drought shortened tempers.

A week after the agent came back to the office, I had finished not only the hundred pages she'd asked for, but an entire first draft of the book.

David had landed a great assignment producing a commercial so I had cash available to Xerox three copies of the manuscript. The two of us waited at the copying office until about eleven o'clock at night. As we drove home, I was unusually quiet. I held the boxes of copies in my lap as though cradling a newborn baby. Suddenly I didn't want to give it up.

As I debated within myself, trying to mull over possible combinations of what would happen if I sent the manuscript to the agent, it became clear to me that I had written my autobiography in the only way I could, which was for myself. I had no constraints from publishers, no censorship and no promise of monetary reward. I had not tried to preserve my adult self-image. On the contrary, I had been candid regarding my shortcomings, foolishness, fear and self-destructive tendencies.

After mailing the manuscripts, I worked in our half-acre yard, trying to save the shrubs and trees by watering them in the evening and early morning, trying not to think about the fate of my book. Without much enthusiasm I also began the search for another job. September was coming to an end and it was still hot. This summer had seemed interminable. My stepson began ninth grade public school wearing shorts and a tank shirt. We were all tired of eating cold salads and barbecued burgers but it was too hot to cook inside.

As I worked in the garden day after day, I kept thinking about the decision my brother and I had made to contest our mother's will. Perhaps it was the current media fad spawned by public disclosure of family disputes after the death of billionaire J. Paul Getty the year before that had generated so much press over the text of Joan Crawford's will. Whatever the reason, Chris and I had to endure public humiliation immediately upon legal filing of the will in New York City.

In fact I had walked into the New York apartment where David and I were staying with friends after the funeral in time to see the local TV newscaster read: "It is my intention to leave nothing to my daughter Christina or my son Christopher for reasons that are well known to them." He went on to say that the two younger siblings had been left trust funds of $77,500 each. Curiously enough, the information on the very first page of the will was not mentioned. No one reported that one daughter alone had been left all mother's personal property and the unpaid interest on the life insurance. Personal property included mother's New York City apartment, the furniture, clothes, silver collection, her jewelry and memorabilia. In addition, mother had belongings and furniture stored on several floors in the Manhattan Storage company. Even though some things, including jewelry, had been disposed of during the last few years, the estate for tax purposes was valued at over two million dollars. The will stated that fifty percent went to five charities, about $100,000 went to various individuals, a trust of $77,500 went to both younger adopted daughters to be paid over a period of twenty years and the rest (after lawyers fees and taxes) went to one younger adopted daughter alone.

When the paragraph about the disinheritance hit the news wire services most papers in the United States carried the juicy tidbit. "For reasons well known to them" became a statement and then a question. What reasons? What unspeakable thing had my brother and I done to cause such rancor?

At the time, both my brother and I were private people.

My first reaction to the will and the media exploitation of it was total shock. I couldn't believe this was happening. Why would anyone do such a thing? My mother was not naive. She had carefully cultivated public attention all her life. She had to know what a sensation the language of the will would cause. If she'd simply wanted to disinherit the two of us, that was her privilege, but did she have to be so cruel about it?

My second feeling was rage. It harked back to the anger and helplessness I'd felt as a child unable to defend myself against the tyranny and chaos surrounding my life.

Once again my brother and I were linked together in a tangled karmic web. I was furious at the cruelty of my adopted mother and the callousness of the press, who chose to single out the last paragraph of the will without reporting the rest of it: that one daughter had been given a vastly disproportionate amount of money not equally shared with her "twin."

I made an appointment with a New York attorney I'd known for many years and asked him if anything could be done. My sense of injustice had also been inflamed. I told him that it was not the money as far as I was concerned, it was the principle. It seemed so unfair to adopt *four* children and make substantial provisions only for one.

It was that sense of injustice and anger that had propelled me. Then one morning I awoke with a terrible feeling of grief. It was like a giant wave smothering me, drowning me alive. The grief was immense. I couldn't think, I couldn't talk. I had no interest in eating. The grief made me feel sick to my stomach all the time. After a few days the tears mercifully came. Why did she hate me so? How could she have pretended for so many years that we had some understanding of each other once I became an adult? How deceitful she had been. Whatever malice toward me she'd harbored in her deepest heart and soul festered there until the day she died.

I asked everybody that had been with her the last few years what the language of the will meant. They all told me they didn't know.

The lawyers told me that it was going to be a tough case. There is no law that prevents parents from disposing of their property as they choose, even in the case of adopted children. Part of the current problem went all the way back to my original adoption. It was usual in the early forties for Hollywood people who adopted children to be required as a part of the adoption proceedings to set up irrevocable trust funds for the child in advance of the adoption becoming final. Even in those days, judges realized the volatile nature of show business stars and their incomes. Joan Crawford was a single woman, twice divorced when she acquired me through a private broker. She had been rejected as a suitable candidate by the Los Angeles County Bureau of Adoption. Therefore, she went to Las Vegas for the court adoption even though she was a California resident and I was born in Los Angeles. There is no record of the judge requiring a trust fund despite the fact that my mother was an unmarried woman. After searching for months, we were still never able to locate any information on where my brother Chris was adopted, if indeed he was ever legally adopted at all.

A lawsuit was time-consuming, harrowing and expensive.

I was torn between wanting justice and wanting to forget the whole mess. A tragedy had finally decided the issue for me. My brother suffered a serious industrial accident. A scaffolding that he was working on had given way suddenly, and he fell twenty feet to the street. His head, neck, shoulders and back had been injured. For several days he was in intensive care. Even when he recovered sufficiently to go home it was doubtful he would ever be able to work full time again. Chris was only thirty-five years old and a Viet Nam veteran.

No matter how dreadful it was going to be, I decided that the will contest was the least I could do to help my brother and his family. If, in the process, we also cleared our personal reputations, so much the better.

There are times in one's life when you have to stand up for yourself. You are left one of two choices: roll over and get kicked in the ass or stand up and fight. We would now fight.

I told the attorney that I didn't want one dime of whatever settlement we were able to get. The money, if there was to be any, would go to my brother and his family.

Having never given testimony at a deposition, I didn't know that the experience is second only to being tortured in the Spanish Inquisition or burned alive at the Salem witch hunts!

Having also never been through a lawsuit I was not prepared for the amount of time eaten away by endless delays and interminable details. Whether your side wins or loses, the lawyers and paper manufacturers are the only true victors of the spoils. One thing becomes enduringly clear: the entire process is set up for those with the most to lose, whether that loss is money or life. It is *not* set up for the individual who perceives she has been wronged.

In the midst of his own physical pain, I heard my brother say that if the situation had been reversed, if the two girls had been left out of the will, he would have split whatever sum of money four ways equally and let us all go on about our lives. There were to be many days in the future when I dearly wished that had been the case.

Los Angeles was still unseasonably warm in October 1977. We were beginning to wonder if the cool weather and rains would ever come.

One morning the Santa Ana winds blew across the valley, hot off the Mojave Desert. I walked outside and sniffed the air for smoke. October was the time for brush and forest fires. This autumn might be a bad one because of the drought. The hills were bone dry and the Santa Monica Mountains stood brown—ready to flash red-yellow-grey smoke into the air.

I was watering some bushes by the house when I heard the phone ring. I set the watering can down on the brick walkway and took the back stairs to the kitchen two at a time. The screen door slammed behind me just as I picked up the phone on the fourth ring.

It was the agent in New York. I was stunned. I sent the manuscript to her only a couple of weeks before. I hadn't expected to hear anything from her so soon.

Her voice sounded evenly modulated but it held a hint of excitement. Since we'd never met, I had no idea what sort of person she was, although she seemed businesslike.

"I have a very good offer on the book for you from William Morrow." She continued giving me details on the offer for both the hardcover and paperback editions.

She spoke rapidly. I knew nothing about the publishing business. I had no idea who this William Morrow was, not even whether it was a person or a publisher. The paperback jargon was also beyond my comprehension so I asked her to repeat the entire thing as I got a piece of paper to write down the information. This time through I understood more, particularly the incredible fact that someone was willing to pay me a lot of money to publish my book.

We talked further only briefly. Again, she told me it was a good deal and recommended that I take it. However, there were lots of other publishers. This one was not one of the biggest but she thought they'd do a good job. If I wanted her to look elsewhere, she said she'd be glad to do so.

I didn't know what to say. David was not home so I told her I'd have to think about it and call her back, maybe tomorrow. She said she'd need to know soon and I promised her I'd call the next day.

It was only when I hung up the phone that I sat down. What an astonishing event. I noticed my clothes and smiled. I was wearing a pair of faded jeans, my stepson's old tee-shirt with Mickey Mouse cartoon characters on it and rubber-thong sandals. My hands were covered with garden dirt and my hair was held off my face with a single large clip. What a contrast to my image of the elegant world of New York agents and publishers. I looked like a migrant farm worker. It was a good thing I had a sense of humor. I was going to need it.

When David returned from work and I told him about the phone call he was as surprised as I had been. As is his custom he asked "What do you think?"

We both laughed. It was too late now to call the agent back in New York. First thing in the morning I would tell her "yes" with the provision that I could meet the publisher before signing the contract. David took me in his arms. His strength felt good. It made the nervousness and anxiety melt away. I never doubted for a moment the validity of the book. My nervousness came from not knowing anything about the people we were dealing with or the business we were on the brink of entering. It was an entirely new world for both of us. Thank goodness we had each other. I didn't think I could do it by myself.

Throughout these first moments of transition from private to public life, another pattern was established subtly and indelibly.

In spite of lifelong evidence to the contrary, during these transition days I thought I wasn't capable enough to accomplish this process of achieving success on my own.

Of course I knew it was my energy and dedication that had created the book word by word. I also knew that it was my friends who had introduced me to the New York agent. I understood it was my talent that the publishers wanted to buy. I realized that it was my writing that would be evaluated by critics and by the public.

If I understood all those elements, why then was it that I didn't believe I was capable of handling whatever else was needed? Why did I try to make David coresponsible for decisions I knew how to make in the first place?

Wasn't this unusual dependency on my part just asking for trouble, when I'd lived my entire life up until now as a fiercely independent and resourceful person? Wasn't that creating the seedbed for future conflict? Didn't that take away some of my feeling of real accomplishment?

The answer to all these questions was a resounding "yes."

Why then did I persist in following this course?

Looking back, I think it was because of the dream. The dream of family, the dream of belonging. The all-powerful dream, the illusion, the magic lantern light show of shadow figures playing out the drama of marriage.

I was afraid that if I didn't involve him, I'd lose him. I was afraid of getting on the skyrocket by myself. Perhaps I'd never get back. Because I'd spent most of my life alone in a sort of emotional solitary confinement, I now needed to take him with me. I didn't know what other choice I might have except this unnatural dependency.

In the midst of trying to cope with my anxiety over losing my husband in the course of this new success, what surprised me the most was that this William Morrow had the courage to publish my book. Even though it was the reality I had lived with all my life, I was aware that most people had always been frightened of that truth, had even denied that truth.

In the 1950s, Confidential Magazine had found out what was going on at Joan Crawford's house and planned a series of articles exposing the events of child abuse that had been witnessed by servants and neighbors, though the words "child abuse" were not in everyday language. That series was never published because mother found out about it beforehand and used her influence through the studio to stop it. Then in 1960 a freelance writer came to me and asked me to coauthor an article on the years of my adolescence, including the problems I'd had with my mother. Together we wrote an article for Redbook Magazine and before it was published mother insisted the article include her side as well. She lied about me by saying I was expelled from Chadwick High School and Redbook printed it. Although they said they didn't believe her, it was the easiest way to avoid a possible lawsuit.

The truth is more than a double-edged sword. It is threatening to those people who live their lives as a fantasy. In hindsight, perhaps I should have insisted my mother tell the truth, and perhaps sued her and the magazine for libel if they failed to do so. But at the time that would have been out of the question. I was only twenty years old living on my own in New York. Ironically, the uproar created by the article eventually landed me an acting contract at 20th Century Fox Studios in Los Angeles.

Before her death mother had ghost writers coauthor two highly fabricated and fantasized books on her life. Now Bob Thomas was writing a biography of her for Simon & Schuster.

Mommie Dearest, however, was not fundamentally about Joan Crawford at all. It was my autobiography. It was the chronicle of my struggles to survive my relationship with my mother and find not only reality but forgiveness toward both of us. It was the first contemporary case history of physical and psychological child abuse amidst a lifestyle of affluence, shattering the myth that family violence occurred only when poverty and ignorance were factors in the equation.

In my writing I had intentionally tried to leave the innocent untouched. However, to the utmost of my ability to remember and with reference to extensive research, I told the truth.

I had lived with that truth for such a long time that it still seemed odd to see it sitting on Xeroxed pages waiting to be discovered by the general public. But there were also hundreds of people in both the entertainment and other businesses who knew parts of my truth from their own personal experiences.

In short, what I had written was *not a secret*. The general story was already known throughout several large communities.

The unique aspect of the book, I thought; was that I had told my story not in retrospect, but through my eyes of a child as it was unfolding, with only a limited understanding of motivation in the world outside that child's own being. The adults in my childhood world never told you *why* things happened the way they did. Those adults never told you why they felt the way they did, *unless* it was somehow your fault!

In 1980 Roy Newquist wrote and had published a book of tape-recorded conversations with Joan Crawford made during the last year of her life. Quoting from his book regarding her relationships with husbands and children she reportedly said: "It's as though I was having such a god-awful time learning my part in my life that I never really had the time to project myself into other people's positions to find out what they were feeling. I'm afraid that through most of my life if you took a simpatico rating on the scale of one to ten, I'd have been a zero. But I tried, I really tried."

My book was not about show business, it was about a child, about a woman, about a mother and a daughter. It was about fear and anger and love. It was about two people locked together for an entire lifetime. It was about violence and tears and loneliness. Always it was from the child's point of view. It didn't attempt to be sophisticated or slick. Parts were raw and gave a sense of discomfort. But that's the way childhood was for me. I went back and got in touch with all that terror, with the chaos. I struggled to put the pieces together and make some strange sense out of all of those crazy years.

I wrote the book to sort out the pieces and tell the truth about life so far. I wrote it for my own benefit. In that sense, I was not so different from lots of other people who keep diaries. I was a lonely person who needed to communicate.

Writing had been the means I'd chosen since I was ten years old. Yet it was strange to think that by publishing this book, I would once again expose myself to the public. The next five years of my life were about to take a radical swing into a new and dangerous orbit.

CHANGING

As the plane came in for a landing over New York City, late in October 1977, I could feel the nervous excitement making my skin tingle. Anticipation mixed with a dread that even though the publisher had said "yes" when I was in California, they'd say "no" after I traveled 3,000 miles to New York.

If the deal didn't go through, I'd be disappointed but it would not be the end of my world. David and I were still young and optimistic about our futures. I'd simply renew my efforts to get a permanent job when I got back to Los Angeles. If these people didn't publish my book, there were other publishers.

The breakfast meeting was set for early the following day in the Edwardian dining room of the Plaza Hotel. Beside myself there were three people at the table. The president and publisher of William Morrow, a pleasant-looking middle-aged New England man, who fit my image of a New York publisher. Next to him was a woman introduced as the editor. She was the one responsible for recommending my book to Morrow for publication. Seated between the editor and myself was the agent.

At the very least, it was a strange meeting. For one thing, these people knew everything about me and I knew nothing about them except their respective business titles. For another, we were talking in such a civilized way about family violence, sociopathic behavior, alcoholism—certainly not ordinary breakfast conversations. Yet to look at the group of us, an outsider would not have guessed at the complexity nor the intensity of our exchange as we helped ourselves to marmalade and coffee cream.

All of these people had read the book. There was general agreement that they all felt it had enormous potential. First the publisher and then the editor indicated the manuscript needed some work. One of them casually asked if I had written it myself or if someone else had helped me.

I almost laughed out loud thinking back over the weeks of crying and sweating in the blistering heat of last summer. Who else would have stuck with it through all that discomfort?

Trying not to reveal how humorously the question struck me, I said, "Every word is my own. I am quite sure that there won't be any problem in my doing whatever revisions and changes are necessary."

Everyone at the table seemed relieved. The next question was about the family photographs. I had brought a few samples from my album with me. They were originally black-and-white but after thirty years had taken on a sepia cast.

I noticed increased excitement on the part of the publisher and the editor when I said, "There are a substantial number of photographs, covering a period of ten or twelve years." We decided on between sixteen and twenty-four pages of photographs as an insert to the book.

After almost two hours, we shook hands. "I look forward to publishing the book," the publisher said. "Call me later at the office," the agent murmured hurriedly. The editor asked, "Can we talk a little longer?"

Over another cup of coffee, we discussed how to go about doing revisions on the book. The deadline for delivery of the final manuscript was April 25, 1978.

Five and a half months wasn't a long period of time in which to accomplish a complete revision of the manuscript, but she assured me it was adequate.

We left the nearly empty Edwardian Room restaurant together and I walked a few blocks down Fifth Avenue with her. She hugged me as we parted company, calling over her shoulder that we'd talk in a couple of weeks.

Suddenly I was by myself amidst thousands of pedestrians in New York City, for the first time realizing it was windy and cold. I was wearing a light blue wool pants suit with a cotton blouse. I hadn't brought a coat.

I pulled up the collar of my jacket and continued walking. How different this visit seemed from the other times I'd been in the city. The streets still looked the same as when I lived there, so maybe I was the one who was changing.

After lunch with a friend whom I'd known since I was eighteen years old, I had an appointment with the attorney handling the will contest. He went over all the documents with me, carefully explaining why they had to sound the way they did and what they were intended to accomplish. It was painful for me. There are two major causes for overturning a will. They are: unsound mind and undue influence. The attorney assured me that we would have to use both.

We have a social custom of parents disinheriting their children as a conscious public punishment, presupposing years of adult discord or perhaps the result of a son or daughter involved in criminal behavior. Not dissimilar from a religious excommunication, disinheritance is in itself an extreme measure because the vast majority of parents wish to see their children do well in the world and want to help them accomplish those goals. "Cutting you out of my will" is issued as a threat in order to try to get children to behave according to the parents' wishes. It is yet another form of control and dominance so prevalent in abusive relationships.

Beyond the punishing social custom, disinheritance is seen as personal animosity, the lack of forgiveness and an unwillingness to make peace at the end of your life. It is a grudge fulfilled.

And now it was going to be challenged. I personally had no doubt that my adopted mother had been mentally and physically ill for a long time. The estate attorney told the family it was suspected that she had cancer but because she was a Christian Scientist, she chose not to be under doctors' care. She stayed at home until she died which was, of course, her privilege.

I read and signed all the necessary papers, knowing they would go on file in the New York surrogate court. As I signed my name, I realized we didn't have much hope because we didn't have much of a case according to existing statutes.

I left the law office emotionally exhausted, only to discover it was now the middle of rush hour and dark. The wind had increased. I couldn't get a cab. After almost half an hour I decided to get on a bus going uptown toward the location of my friend's apartment.

It had been six years since I'd tried to manage public transportation in New York. Each bus that arrived seemed to be more jam-packed than the preceding one that I'd already let go by. Finally it was obvious that there wasn't going to be a bus that wasn't full of people going home from work.

Fumbling for the correct change to drop into the metered glass recepticle, I climbed onto the bus. The doors closed, practically sandwiching the last rider. Although the driver told everyone to move to the back, it was impossible to go anywhere. I held onto a metal oval loop, swaying against the people to my right and left with the motion of the lumbering bus.

The rush hour traffic was as impossible as the conditions on the bus. It took thirty minutes to move twenty blocks. The windows were steamed from the warmth of human breathing. I wasn't used to being crushed together with so many strangers.

Beads of perspiration popped out on my forehead and upper lip. My hands felt sweaty under the dark leather gloves. The back of my neck was uncommonly warm, as though some stranger were breathing on me. Suddenly a trickle of sweat rolled down my cheek. Another trickle ran from my scalp down my back. The perspiration on my lip tasted salty as I flicked my tongue across my mouth.

Sweat was now pouring off my face. I could feel it sticky all over my body.

Surreptitiously I glanced at several people near me. They did not appear to be suffering from the same condition I was. Then I realized that mine was apparently not a normal reaction. Suddenly I was overtaken by a sensation of panic. My embarrassment made the sweating worse. Now my wool clothes were damp and smelled like newly washed sweaters. I had to get away from this crush of humanity. I had to get off that bus!

At the next stop I pushed and shoved my way to freedom.

As the double doors mercifully released me from the bus prison, a blast of cold air hit me, almost knocking me over. All of a sudden I felt like a crazy person, jumping onto the sidewalk, shivering in the wind, yet soaking wet from nervous perspiration. I looked at the street sign and knew there were nine more blocks to walk before I arrived at the safe haven of the apartment.

"Now I'm going to get pneumonia for sure," I thought as I hurried along the darkened sidewalk. No matter how uncomfortable I was on that bus, I should have stayed there until it reached East 80th Street. I tried moving faster but I wasn't used to walking on city pavement and my shoes hurt as they rubbed against my damp feet.

The minute I got to my friend's apartment I stripped off all my clothes and stood under a hot shower. The shower made me feel better but still I didn't stop sweating. After a few minutes, I realized that my condition wasn't going to go away just because I wanted it to stop.

I dried off the best I could and got into my nightgown and bathrobe. It was about seven o'clock. What a strange day, I thought. The end of it was just as unusual as the beginning. Maybe, I consoled myself, it is just the strain of so many changes, so many different attitudes, emotions and events in such a short time. Whatever the cause, I'd never experienced this peculiar combination of anxious feelings and physical discomfort before.

David called from Los Angeles. The sound of his voice calmed me and I told him how much I loved him and what a very difficult day it had been. He understood. "Only one more day, sweetheart," he said, "and then you'll be home."

What I couldn't know at the end of this telephone call was that it wasn't going to be just one more day. It wasn't going to be just another week or another month or even another year. My road home was to be a very long one indeed.

This was the beginning of a new chapter in my life, a chapter that would change my world. A condition would overtake me, not unlike the nightmare that awaited returning Viet Nam war veterans. The condition is called "post traumatic stress" syndrome, and in my case, it almost killed me.

I did not know, nobody else in my world knew, that the pain from my childhood went this far. My life held no warning label to indicate a poisonous childhood could have lethal consequences as my adult life progressed.

I didn't know anything about post traumatic stress disorders, about the flashbacks, the fear, the disorientation, the anxiety attacks so severe I thought surely I would die from them. Unable to breathe, unable to run away, unable to think my way to freedom, I floundered in my own terror, in the quicksand of acute anxiety. I was once again living in hell, only this hell did not come solely from the violence of the past but from now telling the truth of the past as I knew it. This hell sprang from unresolved helplessness. This hell was the condemnation of the victim/child held up to public ridicule and chastisement because of the disclosure of the terrors and the truth of the past.

SHAPING
THE FUTURE

In January, February and March of 1978 a series of events took place that were to shape public opinion far into the future.

On January 17, my editor sent me the following note: "Dear Christina, I thought you would want to see this." Enclosed was a clipping from the New York *Tribune*.

The article was titled: "Auction: 'Joan Crawford Sale'" and had a Cecil Beaton photo captioned "Vintage Crawford ... eyelashes, jewels and a sense for stardom." There were to be three auctions at two East Side galleries. The public would be able to buy an array of items including false eyelashes, costume jewelry, sequined gowns, hats, portraits, scripts, books and letters.

Two of the auctions were at the Plaza on January 19 and February 17 and one was to be at the famous Christie's on March 1, 1978.

The January 19 sale brought in $7,000 for costume jewelry alone, which had an appraised value of only $300.

Four hundred fans got into the February 17, 1978 auction. The New York *Times* covered it and ran photos. To my surprise, one picture featured a sculptured bust of mother which had been done for me and signed "To Christina" with the artist's name and 1941 date.

The New York *Times* said there was a sadness about seeing the things for sale; that people sensed a lack of class in her possessions. Details followed about the hundreds of eyelash sets, the monogrammed sheets, playing cards, film scripts, guest book, the Hollywood memorabilia. Then the reporter said that Crawford felt she owed it to her fans to look and act like a star. That was why those fans were now so eager to buy her belongings. In the course of these peculiar sales, "Miss Crawford had been promoted to kitsch and camp!"

The items, which were appraised at $8,000, brought a total of $42,850.

A follow-up article, "The Selling of Joan Crawford" was done on the New York auction by the Los Angeles *Times* on February 21, 1978. They talked again about the eyelashes and hats, and about the dresses bought by Andy Warhol, a longtime collector of camp, which he intended to use as costumes for transvestites in an upcoming film! "Lawyers for the estate, which consist of many benefactors, including six major charities, say that two adopted children received cash bequests and that one (of them) will receive proceeds of the sale."

The last auction, in March at Christie's, offered the "class" items from the estate, the precious gems as well as gold and silver.

I viewed these three auctions as nothing more than giant public garage sales. The thought of anyone actually selling 250 pairs of new and used eyelashes struck me as a grotesque act.

As I read the various newspaper reporters' words, there

emerged an overall picture of the late Joan Crawford as a woman with indeed "more flash than class." The camp element had infiltrated her later years when she'd made very few movies, and these last so poorly scripted, directed, acted and produced as to become camp items themselves.

Sadly, Joan Crawford had become a caricature of her own stardom, enslaved in its outer trappings of false eyelashes, ankle-strap high-heel shoes, gaudy costume jewelry and luminescent-colored clothing. Oddly enough, she had created this image by herself. In contrast to the early silver screen years in Hollywood when studio press people created her name, molded her image and guided her choice of films, the legacy of the mature years of her life was solely of her own making.

Reading the articles in the winter of 1978 upset me. I found myself feeling embarrassed by my association with her, particularly since she had been the only mother I'd ever known. There was, in these newspaper reports, I thought, the aura of ridicule even though colored by sadness. I did not immediately make connections between the past and future, between personal behavior and public interpretation. Perhaps at the time, the face value of it was unsettling enough, considering that I was in the midst of revealing the inner workings of my own life and past with her.

These auctions focused public attention, eight months after her death, on both the former glamorous stardom and the more recent "camp" elements in Joan Crawford's life. They served as an instantaneous archeological "excavation" under the photographic macro-lens of media scrutiny without benefit of lengthy retrospect.

In the dead of that winter, David and I had to return to New York for my deposition in the will contest and to meet with my editor regarding the third and last section of the manuscript.

The first night we were caught in the blizzard of '78, which closed Kennedy Airport, stranding thousands of people, and shut down the city for several days.

The deposition was one of the most grueling and nerve-wracking experiences I'd ever had. The estate litigator had a habit of snarling and grandstanding, which I later found out was standard procedure intended to dislodge testimony and rattle the opponent. Certainly it gave me a dreadful headache. We started at eight-thirty in the morning and finished about four in the afternoon with an hour for lunch.

I dreaded going back for day two. I felt that everything possible was being done to humiliate me and force such discomfort that I would consider dropping the lawsuit. It did occur to me. But the thought of my brother's condition and the unfairness of the way he'd been treated propelled me forward.

I knew I was telling the truth but that didn't help when the estate lawyer consistently accused me of lying about events. The words of poison and venom that apparently characterized my mother's paranoia as evidenced in the language of the will were being spewed forth by a stranger at the other end of the table.

Ironically, if ever I had doubted the accuracy of my memory as I wrote *Mommie Dearest,* that doubt was forever dispelled by the estate attorneys' behavior and language. Strangest of all, I learned that the disinheritance language went back to a will written in the early 1960s and was language repeatedly carried forward intact through each subsequent document, including the present will which was written only six months before her death.

It was an experience shrouded in surrealism. The very

incidents, the identical feelings that I had just written about in my book were being replayed for me in real life, presented by the estate attorneys. Only now, the opposition attorney and not my mother was saying the words, making the accusations, inferences and criticisms.

It was extraordinarily weird.

In that deposition room, I heard echoes of the childhood litany that began with "bad baby," progressed through ungrateful child, and ended with selfish, willful, stubborn, difficult young woman. It was the litany of *mea culpa*, my fault, always my fault, whatever went wrong, no matter what the circumstances. It made me feel small and immature. It pushed old and very deeply buried buttons of helplessness. And even though I was reminded by my husband and attorneys that I was the childhood victim, it didn't assuage my not-so-deeply-buried childhood fear of being punished or annihilated. It was as though the ghost of my mother had managed to materialize and speak through the mouths of the opposition attorneys who were representing her estate. Their words, even the insulting demeaning intonation they used, were of grisly similarity.

This surreal experience of an interior childhood landscape coupled with the heated external controversy about the book itself produced a precarious entrance to public life created by the publication of my autobiography.

HOLLYWOOD DEALS

THE WHIRLWIND EVENTS preceding actual publication of *Mommie Dearest* were transpiring at such a rapid pace that I could hardly keep up with them. Certainly I had as yet no concept of the ramifications of the various subsidiary rights sales nor what it might feel like to have a movie made about my childhood while I was still very much alive as an adult. I was not prepared for it to go so fast, leaving no time for careful thought or reflection. The book was generating its own momentum as though it were now an entity separate from me, as though I were now almost an outsider to it, a bystander simply watching the parade of events passing by. It felt as though I had lost control over the book, over the process, over how it now affected my life.

When my literary agent needed services on the West Coast for one of her clients, she called on her colleagues in the Los Angeles office.

The film agent assigned to me in Los Angeles was extremely busy the day I had an appointment to meet with him for the first time. He was short with a round face, neatly cut hair. He talked quickly, was constantly on the phone, even when we were in the midst of a conversation in his office.

He said the story would make a great mini-series. Between three phone calls in rapid succession he wanted to know, quickly, what sort of terms I wanted.

It was another five minutes before there was enough silence to voice my answer. I thought he should help with some ideas and suggestions. Nevertheless, I told him I wanted to write the script. The company my husband and I had formed could coproduce, and David, an excellent commercial producer, should be on the film production team.

As that was the end of the time allotted for our meeting, I was ushered out.

I walked to my car, thinking that this meeting was definitely *not* a good omen. I felt that my presence at it had about as much importance as last week's trade papers.

I told David I had a creepy feeling about the entire thing. I wasn't in any big hurry to cope with Hollywood. I had gone to New York to find a literary agent because I didn't think anyone in Hollywood would get this book published the way I wanted it, with the truth of my life as the cornerstone and backbone of the work.

However, less than a week later a call came from the film agent's secretary asking me to come back to meet the head of the television department at the agency. As much as I dreaded it, this meeting was far more civilized. Perhaps because there was someone else in the room, the film agent told his secretary to "hold the calls."

By the end of the meeting I was beginning to think perhaps I'd been wrong. Maybe a mini-series devoting time and care to the parental relationship and the serious problem of child abuse would serve the purpose well.

Just when I was beginning to agree that a TV mini-series might work, I was informed that another agent thought television was all wrong for this project, that it had to be a film!

This agent's influence switched the thrust of the project. Since her office was on the same floor of the agency, after the meeting I walked down to meet her but was told that she was not available.

Once again I went home feeling uneasy. David and I talked for hours about the individual people and the way this project should be done. We talked about who in this town would really understand the book, who would be able to do a decent job with it. There were very few names on the list.

It took another week before the film agent called with initial interest from several studios. I told him that I needed to meet the producers before seriously considering any offers. He proceeded to make the appointments.

I had no idea what would come of these meetings but whatever these men said would give me more information than I'd had before.

The first meeting was with independent producer Marty Ransohoff. I went to the Burbank Studios drive-through gate and there was a parking pass waiting for me. I was nervous going by myself to meet these people. I no longer had the aggressive exterior of an actress. I had forgotten how to make the kind of conversation that assures no embarrassing silence. I was here to listen to what they had to say.

I found the office easily. The secretary was polite. I didn't have to wait long. Marty greeted me with profuse warmth and invited me to sit down.

The producer's office was pleasant but not overly personal. Momentarily another man joined us who represented the Columbia Studio production office. Several times he slipped and called me "Joan" instead of Christina.

Marty was direct and spoke intelligently. Fortunately I was the listener rather than the speaker, so I didn't have to think of things to say to keep the conversation going.

Because the book had not yet been published, I asked if he'd read the manuscript. He said he had just barely had time to read it quickly, which I later realized meant "no."

Then I asked how he envisioned doing the film.

The answer was fascinating. He began detailing an old-fashioned Hollywood extravaganza complete with dancing girls and movie studio backlots. After about ten or fifteen minutes of this description, he arrived at the point at which *my book* actually began.

He stopped to breathe and we three sat in silence. I stared bleakly at my hands folded calmly in my lap. In the prevailing silence I looked up, first at the studio man who called me "Joan" and glowered at me with small dark eyes from beneath lowered eyebrows, and then at the producer. As Marty tried to assess my reaction he seemed to turn his head slightly from side to side as a bird would while hunting down a worm.

"I don't agree," I said quietly. For the first time I said the words publicly that would become an opening statement of mine a thousand times more. "The book is an *autobiography*. It is the story of *my* life, not my mother's." I looked from one to the other in search of comprehension. Neither man seemed to be comfortable.

We exchanged a few more words but I knew the meeting was over. Their fundamental concept of how to turn my book into a film was so far removed from mine that I didn't think there was any chance for compromise. I shook hands all around and departed.

That evening the film agent wanted to know how everything went. I told him briefly about the "dancing girls" and said I didn't think I was interested. Little did I dream that the scenario I'd heard today for the making of *Mommie Dearest* into a film would be very similar to the final product with different producers.

My next meeting was with producer Frank Yablans. Before we met I asked friends about Frank. Everyone knew that he had been the youngest head of a studio when Charles Bludhorn (chairman of parent company Gulf and Western) made him president of Paramount. Now he was an independent producer who had two-picture-a-year deals with both 20th Century Fox and Paramount. It was an unusual situation even for Hollywood. His producer's fee per picture was reportedly $500,000. As a strange coincidence, Frank's former partner was none other than Marty Ransohoff, with whom he'd produced the films *Silver Streak* and *The Other Side of Midnight*.

We were to meet at the 20th Century Fox Studio office. The entire Fox office building had just been redecorated by Dennis Stanfill's wife and looked much more attractive than my previous visit years ago when I was a young actress under contract to this studio to work in an Elvis Presley movie.

Frank Yablans' office was decorated with an elegant color scheme and antiques that looked authentic. Frank possessed an interesting personal style. His monogrammed shirt worn without tie or jacket was casually unbuttoned. He was tan and trim in tailored slacks.

He greeted me courteously, asking me if there was anything he could get for me, such as coffee or a Perrier. I requested the latter.

I watched Frank as he talked easily, wondering whom he

resembled. Then it came to me. When I was nineteen years old in New York, I worked as a night cashier in an Italian restaurant called Pete's Tavern on Eighteenth Street and Gramercy Place. All the waiters and waitresses were Italian and most of the customers were also. My cash register was right next to the bar. My counter was also the same height as the bar so I sat perched on a high-back stool able to look out over all the customers. Because I was so young, a lot of the regulars talked to me and the bartenders joked with me, becoming my pals as well as protectors. It was a great job for a struggling actress. The pay was ten dollars a night plus dinner.

Into this local tavern came a fair share of the New York high-rollers. We had one silver fox who was well known as a big-time bookie from uptown. There were also the numbers men and various collectors for the protection rackets. But during this time I learned that there was a certain kind of New York man who was Italian, dressed expensively, was very charming to ladies and thrived on showmanship that Frank, even though he was Jewish, now brought back to me as an almost forgotten memory.

This man had a ready smile and kept everything going just the way he wanted it. He told me that he saw the film as the story of two strong-willed people and while he certainly didn't want to soften Joan, he felt the film needed to show reasons for her irrational behavior. He then lowered his voice almost to a confidential tone and implied that he'd had similar problems as a child. I honestly didn't know whether to believe him or not. The idea seemed too coincidental to be true, but then nothing was impossible. And as I continued to listen intently to his story, his eyes glistened.

He was personable and charming and convincing. The meeting went well. When it was over, I was left with the feeling the project was out of my control, which was indeed a clue to days not yet unfolded.

The film agent told me the next day that a couple of other producers were expressing interest but none of them could come up with enough money to make discussions worthwhile. That left a man whose name I didn't recognize for my third and *last* interview with producers.

I was to meet him at Paramount, which in 1978 was a sleazy-looking old place in a decrepit part of town given to graffiti and smog. As I was waiting for the little elevator, a man came out of the men's room. I didn't know who he was and he didn't know me either. Of course it turned out that we walked to the same office and he was the producer with whom I had the appointment.

What a tremendous difference in ambiance. We met in what looked like temporary office quarters. The furniture didn't match and there were no paintings or plants. I couldn't help thinking that these quarters were taken just for the day and this interview. There were a few scripts on the desk but no office paraphernalia like pencils or telephone pads. I also got the impression that he was implying he would be partners with the newly ousted president of Paramount when that man worked out his difficulties with the studio. This producer said that he had one picture to do first and then he'd be ready for my film. Of course he agreed that I should write the script and David be one of the producers. "No problem," he assured me.

Personally, I liked him. I just didn't quite understand him. We didn't talk much about how the film should be made because, he said, he usually left that to the creative people. We parted after less than an hour.

As I drove through graffiti-covered buildings in the worst part of Hollywood, from Gower past Sunset, with prostitutes in full view during daylight hours, I thought about the three producers I'd met during the past week. I wasn't sure anyone was right for the picture.

Not one assured me he understood the book and could produce a film that would be true to its intent: to understand the dark side of the human condition and particularly to validate the child's experience of it.

I told the film agent that I wasn't interested in any of the offers of the producers. They just wanted to purchase the book and be done with David and me as far as I was concerned.

Instead of dropping the matter as I assumed he would, the agent instead started talking very fast. What did I want? What more could I ask for? After all, this was my first book and I'd never written a screenplay.

He gave me all the reasons I should step out, but not one reason why I should hold on to what I wanted. My feeling was that he was putting intense pressure on me to take one of the three offers.

When I said very firmly that I wasn't interested and would wait, he immediately suggested that David and I come over to his house on Sunday about eleven where we could talk quietly over coffee.

Wondering what would be accomplished by that, I nevertheless said we'd be there.

Looking back, I realize that was one of the biggest mistakes of my life. My instincts were right. The book wasn't even published yet. Being forced to choose between only three producers and two studios out of the entire motion picture industry at this particular time was not in my best interest.

The book *Mommie Dearest* was going to be a first, unique unto itself. Nothing like it had ever been done before. It was the psychological journey of an abused child, told through the eyes and viewpoint of that child over the lifetime of the parent-child relationship. It was also an expose of the vast difference between the public and private life of a movie star, but that part of the story was not unique. Historically, films about the movie industry had not been successful, nor had they made money at the box office. *Mommie Dearest*, the book, was *not* about Hollywood. It was about two women locked in a thirty-five-year struggle between violence and love.

Instinctively I knew that none of the people to whom I was talking, including this agent, had the vaguest notion of what was crucial to understanding that material.

No matter how much pressure someone applies, there's always the free will to say "no." It is a lesson I will never forget.

I've gone over and over it in my head a hundred times, trying to understand just what happened to weaken my instinct, courage and resolve.

It's difficult to re-create what happened, but once negotiations start, even in a small way, there's an expectation that all parties will continue to play the game through to the end. Win, lose or draw, there's an assumption that you'll play out your hand, you'll not drop out of the race before the winner is declared. An aura of exasperation informs the tone of voice of the person you're negotiating with if you want something other than what's being offered. That tone of voice is meant to remind you that you are not playing by the rules. It reminded me of being a teenager with a well-developed sense of rebellion against authority, and, it seemed to me, I was being treated as though I were now the rebellious teenager without any understanding of how the world worked or what my proper place of gratitude in it was. While I knew that part of my attitude toward them had a lot to do with the fact that I was in over my head in these negotiations, they apparently did not realize this.

At the Sunday-morning meeting, the agent met David for the first time. He drilled my husband about his background and qualifications even though neither he nor the agency intended to sign David as a client.

Once again he asked what we wanted out of this deal. When I told him we wanted to be coproducers, he said we'd never get it. About my writing the screenplay and David being one of the producers, he was a little more positive.

Almost as an afterthought he asked, "Which producer came the closest?"

"I didn't think any of them, as I told you already."

"But if you had to choose . . . which one?"

It was an impossible choice but I said "Frank Yablans."

The agent's eyes brightened for the first time during the meeting.

Immediately, I knew I'd made another mistake. That awful sinking feeling gnawed in my stomach, the feeling of helplessness, of lack of control over the most important matter of my life at this moment. I should have continued to say "no . . . none . . . nothing." By saying anything I was indicating a choice to continue playing the game. The sweat started to trickle down my back.

A few days later the film agent called about five o'clock in the afternoon from New York. I could hear many other voices in the background.

He sounded rushed as usual. Evidently, he'd had a meeting earlier that day with the president of Paramount studios, who was also in New York on his way to the Cannes Film Festival, held in May every year in the south of France.

Paramount had made an offer of $200,000 for the book.

I waited to hear the rest of the deal but that was it. No script, no production job, nothing else.

"That's not enough." I replied. "I'm not interested."

"That's the most anyone's offered, Christina," he said sharply.

"That's okay, I'm still not interested."

He was audibly agitated and went to get the New York literary agent.

She got on the phone and we exchanged minimal pleasantries. She told me that there weren't any other offers and that if I wanted to complete the film deal that I should go ahead and accept this offer from Paramount.

I was told that the president of Paramount was leaving for Europe in the morning and the deal would go away if he didn't have an answer before he left.

This was preposterous. I thought for a moment about saying something about what they could all do with their ultimatum, but instead I just said, "Tell him to have a lovely trip and enjoy the film festival. I'm not interested."

Both agents got upset. They said that I was being unreasonable, that if the deal went away it wasn't their fault and that I would have to exonerate the agency.

"Fine" I said, "you're exonerated! I hope the deal does go away because I don't want it! How many times do I have to tell you I'm not interested?"

In exasperation we all hung up. Initially, I was very annoyed. As the evening wore on and I had more time to think about it, I became furious. This entire thing was turning into a tangle, getting everyone deeper and deeper into the web.

The more I said *no*, the more it seemed to spur everyone on. Everyone was getting mad at me for not wanting what they wanted me to want.

I knew that scripts by new screenwriters were getting the same price as the studio was offering for all the rights to my book, plus my writing the screenplay, plus David's production services. By Hollywood standards where even modestly budgeted films cost eight million dollars, this offer was low, even though to me personally it sounded like a lot of money. Besides, I was still concerned that not one producer had understood what I had written.

A stray piece of gossip was the first indicator that my book was going to be something of a major publishing event. An old friend from New York called to tell us that he just heard the most extraordinary news. It was rumored that somebody had pirated Xeroxed copies of the original *Mommie Dearest* manuscript and was selling these copies for $1,000 each! No one had heard of such a thing before. Something unusual was going on.

From the time that Paramount made its offer on the picture, no other offer on the film was submitted to us. Interestingly, though, all the previous offers to purchase the book outright had been the same price: $200,000.

I had not been around the show business scene in years and never in my previous experience had I been involved in contract negotiations of these proportions. I had no former relationship with any of the people with whom I now dealt, which made it extremely difficult. One word, one alternate use of deal terminology could change the entire thrust of the contractual meaning.

In order to come closer to what David and I had requested, the contract areas were split into different segments at different fees.

However, when I talked to the agent later, he said there was a misunderstanding and that wasn't what Paramount agreed upon. When I told him those were the notes I wrote down during our conversation, he was very angry with me once again.

David and I decided we needed a lawyer. We needed to know that someone was on our side. Under present circumstances, we also felt the need of an independent witness to hear these conversations.

I had not received anything in writing from the agency. We were all discussing the points of the proposed film deal from memory and personal notes.

It was July 1978. The heat and smog hung over the San Fernando Valley. We still lived in the same little house in Tarzana. It was like an oven. David, his son and I spent as much time in the pool as possible.

One afternoon we were all in the pool playing water volleyball when the phone rang. I had set the phone outside on the patio and answered it, still dripping wet from swimming. It was our new attorney. He sounded agitated. He carefully explained that Paramount was threatening to sue me!

"What for?" I asked, thinking this was some weird joke.

I couldn't believe my ears when he told me that Paramount said I was in breach of contract!

"What contract?" I laughed. "There *is* no contract."

Again agitated, the attorney said Paramount claimed that I agreed to less money on the screenplay and now I'd gone back on my word and wouldn't acknowledge the other terms.

"You tell them to go ahead and sue me! If they want to look ridiculous I won't stand in their way. I don't care if there is *never* any picture made out of my book. Tell them to do whatever they want. I don't care."

I realized that I was yelling at the wrong person. However, I began to realize this attorney was also out of his element.

"I'm sorry." I apologized. "I'm so tired of the whole thing.

I wrote down what the agent told me as the terms of the deal. I'm not backing down now because I don't care about the studio or this deal." I hung up.

This should have been an exciting time in my life. I should have felt as though I were reaching success in the big time, like playing cards with the big boys. I did not feel that way.

The people supposedly working with me seemed not to like me very much and everyone else felt like the enemy. If this was success, it certainly had a sour taste. If this was success, it was turning out to be a great disappointment.

Enter Frank Yablans, the white knight in shining armor coming to rescue the deal. Frank made a separate agreement with me and our production company paying the amount in dispute with Paramount. The studio wouldn't back down on their insistence that I'd misunderstood the terms of the deal but they didn't sue me either. Frank Yablans' company made up the difference in order to ensure Paramount got the film rights, and he got the production. The arrangement was effected in order not to kill the deal since the studio was already in the process of announcing to the press that they'd bought the film rights to the book!

A draft deal memo was prepared. After David and I discussed the memo in detail and made notes, he and the attorney went to meet with the agent. By this time there was an air of mutual hostility in our conversation with the agency, a hostility that only fueled the rage that now seemed to surface in me far too easily and often.

David and the attorney proceeded to go over the written memo point by point according to our notes: this was the very first time we'd seen anything in writing and it looked *very* different from the way we'd understood the terms upon hearing them.

On point after point the agent told David that it had been agreed upon already. David replied that this was the first piece of paper we'd ever seen and some of these points had never been mentioned, so how could they have been negotiated?

Finally, the agent threw up his hands in exasperation. Then he uttered the memorable words: *"This is just a deal memo!"* The *real* terms of the contract were still to be negotiated later, following the outline of the memo.

Nevertheless, David persisted. He said the changes had to be made. With that the attorney and my husband left the meetings.

August 3, 1978, on Paramount Inter-communication paper, a revised draft deal memo was drawn up in typical office-memo form for signature by me, David and an attorney in the studio business-affairs department.

On August 8, 1978, a letter of agreement was sent by Frank Yablans Presentations to me guaranteeing the difference between what Paramount paid the company for my screenplay and my original understanding of the deal.

After we received that signed letter of agreement, David and I signed the deal memo in the film agent's office.

No one is to blame for those decisions except me. I had at least two opportunities to walk away. I knew it was wrong from the very beginning and the situation never improved. Neither of my two screenplays were produced and Paramount never negotiated a final contract.

What compounded the many real difficulties and misunderstandings in these negotiations was that I took them personally. It all felt like an attack by the enemy, not a matter of doing business.

It hadn't yet dawned on me that all of this was just a game. Business was a game. Negotiations were game strategy. Nothing was intended to be personal about any of it. The other side was more experienced in the game-playing. Even when I was confident in my ability to negotiate from a position of strength, there was no sense of accomplishment. For me the negotiations felt like another battle with an old enemy. That enemy wanted to take from me, not give to me. That enemy generated at that time a deep, ancient feeling of being cheated, of being manipulated, of being used.

How you played the negotiations game, what you were willing to do in order to win, the amount you were forced to give up in order to get a deal—I didn't realize then, but I do now, that it was all just a game. There was no right or wrong, no good or bad.

I had fallen into an old trap of making judgments on both the people and the process, viewing them from the perspective of my own past human interactions, instead of recognizing them as instruments of present business strategies.

Interestingly, months later Frank Yablans, who knew that the final price of the deal was more than double the original offer, told me I'd done a hell of a good job negotiating—for a beginner. He said it with a tone of approval.

I suppose he meant that as a compliment. But at the time it was too close, too personal, too tied up in my old fears—and I could not sit back and look at these events with any professional perspective. Those negotiations served only to stir up my anxiety about the publication of my life story, an anxiety about whether or not I would be understood, an anxiety which would eventually overtake my life.

IMAGES

NOT LONG AFTER signing the Paramount deal memo, I went to New York for the publisher's sales conference. The list of books to be published that fall was being presented to the salesmen and there was a luncheon afterwards at which I was to be a guest of honor.

New York City in the month of August is humid and hot.

It was another strange combination of events. First I had to make a little speech at the sales conference which made me extremely nervous. Everyone sat around a very long table with all eyes staring at me. The room was packed with editors, staff, sales people and executives. I didn't quite know what was expected of me and I hadn't prepared anything. So, I managed to say something brief and hoped it was adequate. Afterwards, everybody said it was terrific and that my book was sensational. The publishers seemed delighted.

Two days later I had to appear for further deposition in the will contest. The estate attorneys insisted that I give them a final version of the manuscript, which I didn't have, because the galley proofs were with the publisher and the book was in the process of being printed. Mercifully, this session was less than half a day. Perhaps it was the heat.

In the end, the elderly judge who had been appointed as guardian ad litem for the minor grandchildren extended his hand to me as I stood to say good-bye. We shook hands and he said "Good luck with your book. I hope you make a million dollars ... you deserve it."

There was an audible gasp from the three estate attorneys and a collective look of shock on their faces. David and I couldn't help laughing at such unexpected candor in the midst of the harassment. My attorney tried to cover his delighted smile with the back of his hand even though his eyes twinkled.

That same week the publishers had scheduled my first public interview. The writer agreed to wait until publication date nearly two and a half months away before releasing the article. He was part of a group of independent journalists known as the Writers Bloc. I was impressed that he was so well prepared and had obviously read the book. When I asked him about that, he told me that the publishers had given him an advance galley proof to read in their office.

He had a tape recorder and took notes also. We talked fairly easily after the first few minutes. It was a great relief to have the first one go so well.

It was during this same see-saw trip that we saw the current issue of Viva magazine with a Helen Lawrenson article titled: "The Troubling Truth about Joan Crawford—A life more bizarre than any screen role." The article was excerpted from her upcoming book.

Helen Lawrenson wrote about the "blue" movies ... one of which was called *The Plummer,* made with comedian Harry Green. It was a silent film with subtitles. During her first marriage to Douglas Fairbanks, Jr., my mother bought every print with one exception. That exception was owned by the Quiet Birdmen of America, a private club of aviators of which Lindberg was a member. After talking about the problems in the relationship with her fourth husband, Alfred Steele, and with her children, the article went on to say that "Anyone who didn't know how Joan treated them would have said that they were four lucky kids. In reality their childhood and adolescence were wretchedly unhappy."

Helen Lawrenson visited with Joan Crawford in June 1956. This article in *Viva* magazine was published in August 1978.

As I read the article, I was astonished to realize, once again, how much of the truth about my mother and our real life behind the scenes was known. At the time, of course, practically nothing was done to spare me the pain and humiliation of my childhood.

But a deeper anger was beginning to stir inside me, an anger that would erupt like a volcano when my publicity tour began. As I began to realize that some members of the Hollywood community, of the press, and segments of the public were not going to side with the child victim, I was shocked. When it dawned on me that they were, in fact, going to blame the victim for having written the book exposing the torture and trauma of child abuse, I was outraged.

Mommie Dearest had *not* been published yet nor had any of the book's serializations appeared. Yet, this article contained substantial additional information about what happened in our house and as far as I knew, it was all true. Therefore, much of what was soon to be released in my autobiography was already published information, widely available. Many people in the Hollywood community and elsewhere knew the facts because they had lived them when the events were actually happening. That knowledge would come back to haunt me on the national book tour as I fought to preserve my own sanity and courage.

RAGING
CONTROVERSY

MOMMIE DEAREST ENTERED the New York *Times* best-seller list at number five in the fall of 1978. Two weeks later, it hit the number-one position and held that place for several months. In fact, *Mommie Dearest* stayed on the New York *Times* best-seller list for forty-two weeks. The publishers were printing and shipping books as fast as modern technology permitted. In six months the hardcover sold over 500,000 copies. The book club edition sold one million. The paperback eventually sold about four million copies.

It is my belief that *Mommie Dearest* originally got through "the system" and into the mainstream of public awareness because no one understood what the book was about. The deeper implications escaped them. Most people thought the story was another biography of a movie star with some graphically sensational material, which provided an old format with a new twist. Interestingly enough, celebrity biographies at that time usually did not make the best-seller list. They usually did not generate a strong enough audience to have great financial success either.

At publication the world as I knew it blew up in my face. All hell broke loose. Instead of the tailored wool suits and turtleneck sweaters I wore on my book tour of ten cities, more realistic outfitting equipment for this trip should have been a military flak jacket, survival rations and fixed bayonets. The fighting controversy was intense.

I arrived alone in New York and stayed with friends in the city for a few days while David finalized the purchase of a new house for us in Los Angeles.

I was nervous about being on television, being a public person again. It dawned on me that something totally unexpected and rather unpleasant was happening.

The first official interview of the tour was held in the publisher's office with a reporter from *Women's Wear Daily*. I felt as though I were being put on trial.

The finished piece suggested that what I had done in writing the book raised questions of ethics, kindness and exploitation on my part.

Apparently I was not being criticized for what I said about my mother because others had said it either before or were in the process of saying it simultaneously. What I was being criticized for was telling the truth, in public, about what happened between the two of us, mother and me. That was a story that had not been told in modern times. A child had never risen up against the parent to expose the violence, shame, guilt, and struggle for absolute power between them, over the course of a lifetime.

Many times I would be reminded that what I had written was actually a mirror in which every reader would see some part of themselves. Precisely because I had written through the eyes of a child and because every reader had once been a child, it was impossible for people not to relate emotionally. The "book-mirror" I had created was the reader's own childhood and the emotional reaction was a reflection of unfinished issues the reader had with his or her own parents.

However, more often than not, *I* was accused of writing the emotions the readers *felt* while reading my book, not the emotions I actually expressed in the pages of the book.

Strangely enough, what I did best as a writer, which was to connect people with their own feelings, temporarily backfired on me. It was clear from reading both articles and reviews on *Mommie Dearest* that many of the reporters and reviewers became so caught up in their own emotional reactions to the child/parent relationship in the book that they could not separate their feelings from mine. So, the two sets of feelings, theirs and those I had written about in the book, were intermingled and came out in the newspaper pieces intertwined if not entangled.

Anger is an emotion that is hard to cope with under almost any circumstance. In 1978, the press was not prepared to write about a child's rightful anger or despair over harmful, destructive parental behavior toward her when she, as a child, was helpless, powerless.

Some of the press then gave other reasons why I really wrote *Mommie Dearest*. Some told the public that I did it for money.

Others said that I wrote the book for revenge. At first I thought they meant for being disinherited. Later I understood that they had a deeper revenge in mind. They interpreted my telling the truth as a way of "getting back" at what had been done to me. They were wrong about that but at least their logic made a little more sense. Revenge does imply that a punishable act has been perpetrated which deserves retribution. But the way it was discussed in many articles and reviews, "revenge" sounded as though I was a spoiled child who tattled. Why was it so difficult to believe that someone could be motivated by a desire to tell the truth and dispel an injustice? Was it wrong to defend oneself? Why need there be ulterior motives?

In retrospect, it occurs to me that media professionals were not taking time to think the problem through. They used old concepts to confront new ideas. In the process they confused the issue of disclosure by identifying me with it, rather than seeing disclosure as a process which every victimized child eventually experiences. They confused the issue because I told the truth, and that truth was the disclosure which the interviewer called "revenge."

The second day of the book tour I stopped an interviewer and said, "Aren't you asking the wrong question?" The interviewer stared at me blankly.

"The question is not really why I chose to share my experiences with other people. The question we should be dealing with is why does anyone mistreat their children? I think that's what we should be talking about."

I soon learned, however, that *the public understood*. Millions of them had lived their own private version of my story and letters from them now poured in by the hundreds.

But was there an underlying fact that was beginning to unravel? Is it possible that I was touching the raw nerve of a secret assumption more prevalent than anyone had previously realized? Was pressure on that raw nerve starting to cause massive public anxiety? Perhaps it was. Otherwise the hostility that initially greeted me made absolutely no sense.

Why wasn't it the reverse, I wondered? Why wasn't the outrage focused on the person who had hurt the child rather than on the child who was trying to tell the truth and be understood? Why wasn't the sympathy on the side of the child? I was confused by this reaction.

The first television interview was with Jane Pauley of the NBC "Today" show.

David was standing just offstage, within sight but engulfed in shadow. Beside him was the public-relations woman from the publishers.

We were on the air. Jane's first questions were centered on why I wrote the book.

Try as I might to stay focused, and although my voice answered reasonably clearly, my mind was fading into an old, hidden place of safety, a place withdrawn from the pain and the anger.

I felt I had not done well, that I was visibly nervous and defensive. David tried to reassure me, for which I was grateful even if it was a deception.

There wasn't much time to think before appearing on another TV show with a live audience and a panel of experts on child abuse.

One man in the audience said in an agitated tone of voice that his dad had beaten him lots of times when he did something wrong but he didn't consider those beatings child abuse because his dad said they were for his own good. Then the man said. "And I know my father loves me!" With this, he was close to tears and sat down.

There was an awkward silence.

"There is never an excuse for beating a child in order to discipline him," I said quietly. "I'm sorry to tell you that what you experienced was child abuse, physical abuse from your father who was probably also beaten when he was a little boy."

The panel of experts was left to pick up the pieces and the half-hour show was over.

My schedule was booked solid. We went from one studio to the next without stopping to rest or reflect.

By the end of the first day I recognized a pattern to the questions being asked by the interviewers. That pattern had been formulated over the previous months by a series of seemingly unrelated events. It became a pattern by the eerie phenomenon of the news media feeding on itself. Once an item breaks on the wire services, you can turn to any network, any news station, and hear similar reports of the same event.

Portions of the most sensational material from the book, such as the terrifying "night raids," were published earlier in New York magazine. So, every interview had questions about the night raids. Almost every interviewer asked about Hollywood's reaction because it had become a guarantee of publicity for some Hollywood celebrities, to make remarks about me and my motivations *or* what a wonderful woman they had known my mother to be.

The truth was that the Hollywood of my childhood knew exactly what was going on in my home. The difficulty these celebrities faced now was the fact that years ago almost no one had confronted mother with her behavior because if they had, she dismissed them as friends or employees.

Today, the community was defensive not only because of their own past behavior but also because of the old Hollywood system which often protected movie stars from personal responsibilities as well as from public disapproval.

What bothered me most was that very few people who knew I was telling the truth were given equal time to be heard.

Initially newspapers published many primarily anti–*Mommie Dearest* letters or articles. In fact, in the very early days of the book's release, before the public had an opportunity to actually read what I'd written, several reporters associated with major newspapers in Los Angeles and New York told me that judging by the similarity of the letters, there seemed to be an organized letter campaign against me, almost, they said, like political form letters given to people to copy in their own handwriting, or merely to sign.

Apparently that campaign lost steam quickly and either disappeared or went underground.

What upset David far more were the death threats. The publishers had never experienced any situation like this, so they spoke to David, wondering how to handle both the information and the security precautions on the tour.

It was a terrible responsibility for my husband, the first of many that were to haunt him over the coming years.

He made the decision not to tell me and to have the publishers open all the mail, censoring it before sending it along to our home.

He also decided that to have visible bodyguards or conspicuous security might escalate the situation. David took a big risk. If the threats were just intended to shut me up and send me home, then I was not in any physical danger. If, on the other hand, there were adults out there who had focused on me, blaming "the messenger" for awakening in them the knowledge of their own lifelong "bad news," then chances were greater I might be in real danger.

Russian roulette.

The decision he made was the right one. The threats stopped fairly quickly and no one but David and the publishers knew about them at that time.

In the meanwhile, David was constantly beside me wherever we went, no matter what the circumstances. He was in all the studios, at all the interviews, in all the meetings. He always made sure we had a way to enter and exit buildings through a nonpublic access. There were always others who met us and stayed with us at all times. I was never left alone except to go to the bathroom.

For the moment, my husband had no other life. He had become my guardian protector, as well as my best friend, my only confidant.

Strange to say, I was such a "hot issue," I dared not say anything "off the record" to anyone except David. As my face and my name became the center of national controversy, I found myself being cut off from any casual contact with friends or even family.

Our son was left at home with a black belt karate master while we were on tour. We were deeply concerned with his safety.

It wasn't long before I guessed that David's hypervigilance was not just ordinary concern for my comfort. Finally he told me about the death threats.

God—it was awful. Not one moment to relax, not one kind word from the press, scared each moment I was in public that some stranger would try to kill me.

When we arrived at one of the TV shows we met a nice man who introduced himself as Dr. Vincent Fontana. He was an early pioneer in the child-abuse field, a physician, and had written one of the first clinical books on the battered child. Dr. Fontana had been asked to appear on the show, as had other professionals on other programs to give some credibility to my appearance on a topic so controversial it had *never* been discussed as a national public issue before.

While I was being interviewed Dr. Fontana told David that no one ever wanted to talk about child abuse and that I'd done more than anyone in the past few months to bring the issue before the public.

David told me what the doctor had said on the way to our

next TV show with Stanley Siegel, but there was no time to reflect on the implication. We'd been told that Stanley was a bit controversial himself. He had a way of conducting the interview like a drill sergeant with the audience as his review board.

About six different ways he hammered questions at me, wanting to know if I had loved and if I now missed my mother, since she was dead!

Each time I answered as seemed appropriate to me but evidently not what Stanley wanted to hear because all of a sudden he walked *off the set,* leaving me sitting alone on the stage facing an audience on a live show.

That was a first for me. At first I was horrified. Then I laughed, seeing how preposterous the whole situation was. Fortunately I'd been an actress in theater, TV, soap opera and film for almost fifteen years. Some things you never forget, like how to keep the show going no matter what happens. So, when I composed myself, I asked for questions from the audience and got them.

The next city on the tour was Washington, D.C. It was Wednesday night when we arrived at the elegant Madison Hotel, which was more formal than the St. Regis we had just left in New York.

After being shown to our suite, I noticed copies of both Washington newspapers on the desk.

Since each had insisted on sending a reporter to interview me in New York, I was curious to see if one of the interviews had appeared.

Yes. Both had written *full page* articles on me, but as I read paragraph after paragraph my curiosity turned to anger and exploded into fury. I threw the paper across the room.

My temper subsided as nervous exhaustion flooded

through me, falling as tears. My body was shaking. The feeling of betrayal carried with me from early childhood welled up in my throat all over again. I was enmeshed in my same lifelong struggle to face this pain so I wouldn't have to cover it with all this anger.

I reread parts of the article that spoke of me as behaving as though I were "deprogrammed" and the book as being filled with "intense revenge."

"David." My voice sounded unintentionally imperious, particularly since I really felt like an abandoned child. "You'll have to call the publisher and tell them I'm *not* going on with this tour. I'm not going to defend myself, I'm not going to answer any more questions. I'm just not going to do it!"

I paced back and forth across the room. My heart was pounding. Breath came in spurts. My head ached and my throat was constricted, dry and uncomfortable.

"David—please—call them! *I WANT TO GO HOME!*"

He called the publicist at home. She talked to me, pleading with me to continue, saying she understood how upset I was, that she didn't blame me a bit, that it was very unfair.

She asked me to take some time to relax and decide in a few hours. David and I would have dinner and call her back. Needless to say, she had good reason to be in a panic. *Mommie Dearest* was selling faster than they could print and ship new copies. Everybody wanted to interview the author. The only problem the publicist had was allocating enough hours and saying no when she couldn't fit in the request.

This telephone call could bring all that to a crashing halt with unending professional nightmares for the publicity department.

David took me downstairs to the hotel restaurant. We were seated at a quiet table by the window and ordered a light meal, fish, as I recall, and a glass of white wine.

Sipping on the wine, looking at my distraught husband across from me, I seriously wondered what strange set of circumstances brought us both into this moment together.

This tour and my notoriety was not fun, not glamorous, not filled with exciting adventure. It was excruciating and exhausting.

My dinner arrived. The food looked delicious, artfully arranged with beautiful little vegetables surrounding the fish. The plate resembled an abstract still life painting.

My stomach felt pangs of hunger. It was probably approaching nine-thirty at night. One forkful of fish went into my mouth and I managed to swallow it. The second forkful seemed to send strange messages of closure to my throat which refused to open again and accept anything coming down it.

With a sigh of resignation my fork took a permanent place on my plate beside the uneaten food.

"I can't eat."

"Try, a little, Christina. You haven't eaten anything since breakfast."

He sounded like a patient parent talking to a difficult child.

The waiter appeared. "Is anything wrong, madam?" he inquired with concern.

Trying to appear nonchalant and forcing a weak smile, I replied "No—everything's lovely. Thank you. I'm just not hungry."

He took my plate away and David had the annoyance of me watching him eat by himself.

Apparently, I couldn't talk either, so we sat in awkward silence while David finished his meal.

As we left the restaurant my husband put his arm around me.

"Feel like taking a walk?" he asked kindly.

The November night air was cold. The streets were empty. Unlike New York, there were no other pedestrians.

We walked down a few blocks and turned left, finding ourselves crossing in front of the Russian Embassy, which was ringed with floodlights, bristling with uniformed guards.

Once in the normal shadows again, our conversation continued.

"I can't go on with this, David. It's making me sick. You know it's making me sick. Why would you try and convince me to continue? The whole thing is a replay of my entire childhood, only now that my mother is dead, the media is taking her place. I can't win here. Everyone acts like I've done something wrong. They keep looking for the fatal flaw in me that made my mother hate me."

When privacy allowed me this much honesty, my heart started beating faster and a feeling like fear came over me. Fear and anger—the primary emotions of my entire existence.

"I'm tired of explaining, tired of trying to be calm and rational. I'm sick to death of educating, defending, constantly drawing attention to the reality that there are many others today who need help.

"Why doesn't anyone seem to care? Why do they want to crucify me? All I did was tell the truth. I'm not interested in revenge. I am not a crusader. I do not want to take on the responsibility for changing the whole damn world. I just want to be understood."

My book was a statement of realignment between fact and fantasy. The great irony was how many were now trying to discredit the *reality*. Evidently they wanted to retreat back to the safety of the fantasy, to pretend the truth wasn't so, to pretend there weren't millions more like me.

If there really were millions of us adult survivors of childhood abuse, then the time was right for an uprising, a rebellion of magnitude, a change in consciousness that could ignite a new social movement.

Millions of us could change our world if we could unite. Millions of us could find justice and compassion.

David and I were walking in a large circle, going back to the hotel when we found ourselves standing in front of a small church. It had a painted wooden door, a minuscule patch of yard with a picket fence. It was an unlikely sight to find near Embassy Row and the Madison Hotel. We stood in silence taking it in, wondering what it meant.

"David, I know what you're saying. I understand the responsibility but I want to go home. Tomorrow."

He took my hand and touched my face. "If that's what you want, that's what we'll do. I'm not trying to convince you of anything, I just want you to really think about what going home tomorrow will mean."

"Defeat?" was my first thought. "I can't take the controversy? Somehow, they're right and they've won?" I asked.

He said nothing, just listening to me wander into the abyss.

"Is it like giving up? They win by default because I won't fight?"

A chilling gust of wind caught my hair, scratching it across my cheek, yet beads of perspiration gathered on my forehead.

"Remember what you've been telling people about the children today who need help." David said quietly.

All I wanted in this world right now was permission to go home. I was frightened and angry and disappointed about the world in which I lived.

"Remember the children...remember the children..." echoed in my head.

Was he right? Could I possibly make any difference? I felt so small, so vulnerable right now. It was inconceivable to me that my voice could change things, that one person alone could turn the tide in favor of the children.

"David, if I go ahead with this, it has to be different. I can't play the polite 'let's pretend' game anymore. So— they'll see my anger. They'll see a lot of anger. What happens then?"

"I don't know. I've never been here before," he answered plainly.

"Please God, help me," I asked quickly at the closed doors of this little church. "Help me, give me strength, remember the children."

We walked silently back to the hotel.

The tour did continue. But, the next morning on the Washington, D.C. TV talk show, I launched an attack on the reporters who hide behind their newsprint and misrepresent the seriousness of the problem of child abuse by attempting to discredit me personally.

Now I used the figures. The statistics, the case histories.

One million children a year abused. Problems with drugs and alcohol. Sexual abuse. Generational abuse. Learned behavior that can be unlearned.

Now they could attack me and I could answer with information on a national epidemic affecting all of us. I had turned an invisible corner, which I never felt was totally my choice. But my whole life was on the line. So, I would fight. The world would now see my anger, feel my outrage. I was still scared to death, but the line of safety had been crossed. I saw life as a soldier sees a war from which there is no escape.

TOUR
OF DUTY

AFTER WASHINGTON, WE went to Boston and had a lovely, quiet room at the Ritz Carlton overlooking the Boston Commons.

Boston was also weird, but funny. We were at a TV show, waiting in the green room with two other guests—a fat lady with a giant blue velvet cape who was showing a miniature doll house, and a large trained goose who after performing was picked up by two butchers with blood on their white uniforms. Later that day we were informed that one of the newspaper women interviewing me at lunch didn't want my husband present at our table but he could sit in the back of the dining room.

I cancelled the interview when the woman refused to change her mind.

Cleveland was next and a welcoming change of pace. The TV interviews were great. The interviewers had read at least part of my book and they understood what I was saying. At this point I expressed my gratitude on the show.

How very odd I thought that Cleveland understood both my book and the much larger social problem to which it related when New York, Los Angeles and many points in between appeared not to get it at all.

By the time we got to Chicago I was getting laryngitis. No wonder. When we arrived that night I was taken straight to Irv Kupcinet's TV show, which we taped starting at about ten P.M. I'd known Kup since my childhood and had seen him in the years when I played Chicago theaters as an actress.

So tonight we talked about a past we both knew very well. Only now I was an adult, not a child. He was kind and blunt almost simultaneously. Since he had information and personal experience with our family not included in the book, and he had been a newspaper man for many years, his questions were interesting to answer.

"If it's Chicago, it must be the Ritz Carlton at the Watertower." I tried to joke with David in the elevator around midnight.

The hotel lobby is located on the 12th floor in a giant atrium. Our suite was on a floor in the 20's with a magnificent view of Lake Michigan!

I was exhausted, my laryngitis was getting worse and I had a lot of anxiety about being the *only* guest on tomorrow's Phil Donahue show.

David was getting half crazed taking care of me, my anxiety seizures, my fear of heights in every hotel and my constant (though now unspoken) desire to go home.

In an attempt to lighten up the ponderous seriousness of this trip, he did a very funny, very silly comedy routine about the adult toys in the bathroom of this very chic hotel.

First there were the little bottles of lotions, potions and

shampoos, then there were caps and bags and polishing rags. Finally there was the bidet.

He was so silly and funny doing his "Gol-ly...I'm just a good-ole country-boy" routine, that I laughed and forgot the days of pain and frustration.

We made one gigantic mistake, however. We put David's shoes outside the door to be polished overnight in what is more commonly a European hotel tradition. The next morning about seven A.M. I opened the door to our room and saw only a size 10 pair of women's sandals in the hall-way. No shoes for David. I called housekeeping who referred me to hotel security.

What David didn't tell me until now was that they were the only pair of shoes he had packed for this three-week trip.

A few minutes later the doorbell rang and a house detective appeared who looked as though he'd been recruited from the defensive line of the Chicago Bears football team.

I told him the sad story, handed him this giant pair of ladies' sandals and closed the door.

David was now threatening to go to the Phil Donahue Show in his stocking feet!

Great, I thought. This is just great! Here we are trying to make some sense out of what seems to be total chaos all around us, and David loses his one and only pair of shoes! If it had been a little later in the day we could have gone to one of the stores in the hotel building and bought him another pair. But we were supposed to leave at eight A.M. Nothing was open yet. I was getting annoyed.

"Why didn't you pack another pair of shoes?" I asked in a pique. It was a stupid question, designed, I guess, to make me feel better because it certainly didn't accomplish anything else, except to put David even more on edge.

Attack, attack, that's all I knew any more. Well, that was the state in which I found myself constantly. Little wonder I couldn't eat, couldn't swallow, afraid I would choke to death.

The doorbell rang again and this time the house detective was holding a pair of men's shoes, however, not the ones that belonged to David.

"You're getting close," I said, sounding more sarcastic than intended. "Maybe that man has my husband's shoes. Please keep trying! We have to leave *very* soon."

Room service breakfast had arrived but as usual after two or three bites, I couldn't get my throat to open and swallow the food. Sometimes I was even hungry and still couldn't eat. So I drank my coffee and took my vitamins with some orange juice.

The doorbell rang a third time. The beaming house detective truimphantly held up David's shoes! It was really miraculous work, considering both the size of this hotel and the limited amount of time. We thanked this man profusely.

Phil Donahue was extremely well prepared and one of the very few hosts who had a pre-show session with his guests. It was very helpful and reassuring to me for many reasons. It gave me a chance to get used to how he spoke in person as well as letting me know that he had read the book or at least had been very thoroughly briefed.

One hour, all by myself facing three cameras, sitting on the edge of the stage, answering questions fired from Donahue, the studio audience and the call-in audience, felt like an eternity to me.

However, that one show generated hundreds of personal letters in addition to thousands of books sold. At the time Donahue was considered the most powerful television pro-

gram on the air when it came to generating public awareness on issues.

It bolstered my spirits enormously to read Jill Robinson's
review of *Mommie Dearest* in the Chicago *Tribune*. Jill had
grown up in Hollywood and had written a best-seller herself
called *Bedtime Story*.

She understood that mine was not a Hollywood book. She
wrote about it in terms of issues, the oppressed, battered
child trying to win the love of a mother who was also
abused. She called the book "a position paper of child liberation—for some system of appeals which children might go
to for support and protection." She recognized the central
role of alcoholism and the continuing ignorance with which
society deals when confronting that disease.

The review ended on a note of hope, saying "Christina
Crawford has grown to sanity, maturity, and understanding.
She has demonstrated that there is a way out. That is the
importance of her story."

At last someone understood! At last someone spoke out.
Maybe the invisible tide was actually beginning to turn.

Two days before Thanksgiving, we arrived in Minneapo-
lis. After the interviews the next night, when we were ready
to leave, a blizzard hit. All flights were cancelled. David and
I were marooned in the airport cocktail lounge along with
hundreds of other morose travelers.

Eventually the storm lifted and around midnight the
planes were taking off again. We finally did get home early
Thanksgiving Day morning.

David's son was spending the holiday with his mother. My
husband and I went up to Braemar Country Club for dinner by ourselves.

It seemed so lonely and strange. Just one year ago in our
other little house we'd had twenty people for Thanksgiving

dinner. We'd had to borrow extra chairs, plates and silverware from the neighbors. We even borrowed some money from a friend. The book contract hadn't yet been signed and we didn't have even enough to pay our bills. But everyone had fun and we felt companionship.

Now, a year later, David and I had enough money but were all by ourselves. Strange how life plays itself out.

Thanksgiving holidays concluded, my book tour continued with Los Angeles, San Francisco and San Diego.

Marcia Seligson's review for the Los Angeles *Times* syndicate had created more controversy in my own hometown. By now, part of the controversy centered on the fact that this reviewer thought I was telling the truth and expressed that radical viewpoint in print! Then she followed up by questioning why no one intervened to stop the parental behavior years ago.

Seligson talked about the issues of terror, sadism and alcoholism, confirmed by others such as Bob Thomas in his biography of my mother. She recognized that my struggle for my mother's love was "the most fascinating psychic revelation of this gothic tale."

The New York publishers had hired the West Coast public-relations firm of Allen/Rolantz to handle press in California. It was a fortuitous and validating experience to work with Jay Allen, a tall, cranelike middle-aged man, the ultimate traditional P.R. guru. Jay had a long career in entertainment P.R., creating movie stars during Hollywood's golden years at the studios in the 1930s, promoting rock stars in the 60s, and selling books and authors for East Coast publishers in the 80s.

He greeted me by saying he'd known and worked with my mother.

Good, I thought sarcastically. Just the right person to help me with *Mommie Dearest* in Los Angeles!

My initial trepidation was unfounded. Jay and his partner, Lelia, did a great job and were lovely, caring people.

In fact, between interviews at the Beverly Hills Hotel one day, Jay told me about an incident of my childhood he'd personally witnessed that did not appear in the book. It was morbidly fascinating to hear details from his perspective of an incident I vividly remembered.

Jay was doing a post—World War II children's charity campaign for the March of Dimes in the 1940s. Everyone working on the project was invited to a meeting at my mother's house because Joan Crawford was national campaign chair that particular year.

Jay remembered that I was about six or seven years old and my brother approximately four.

Apparently my brother and I were playing in another part of the house that afternoon while the adults gathered in the formal dining room to view the campaign artwork, which was spread out on the large dining room table.

While they were working, they heard some faint sounds like children laughing and then heard at least one child's voice crying.

Mother sent someone to find out what was going on.

The governess brought me into the dining room. Jay said I looked frightened and stood quietly with my eyes riveted to the floor.

Mother asked the nurse what happened. She was told that Chris and I were chasing each other through some of the upstairs rooms and as I closed a door behind me to halt his progress, my brother's fingers were accidentally caught in the door. Of course that made him cry. The nurse hurriedly added that she'd made me apologize to my brother, which I had done. Chris had a few bruised fingers but evidently no broken bones.

In front of everyone working on the children's charity campaign, mother suddenly grabbed my arm and dragged me to the dining room doorway. The sliding door was already open. She forced my hand against the door frame, then slammed the door on *my* fingers.

I screamed! Tears flooded down my face. Not only was I deliberately hurt, I was intentionally humiliated in front of a dozen people.

When Jay finished this vivid eyewitness account, David's first question was, "What did you do?"

Jay looked very sad. "I excused myself and threw up. Then I left the house."

"Didn't anyone say anything to Crawford?" my husband asked incredulously.

"No, I don't think so, at least not while I was there," Jay answered quietly.

"See! That's just what I've been trying to explain for years!" I blurted out. "People *did* know, they *heard*, they *saw* for themselves. This town sure as hell did know!"

"My God, Jay, how do you feel about working with Christina now?" David asked pointedly.

I was so moved by his story that I didn't hear exactly what he answered but got the feeling that there was some poetic justice to this situation, although filled with irony. His story echoes in my mind to this day.

After touring San Francisco and San Diego, we took a break for the Christmas holidays.

We'd actually bought the house David had seen months before and were scheduled to move into it the end of January 1979.

But, as soon as we'd moved, we were on the road again

for the second phase of the next ten-city tour throughout the South and Southwest.

Before we left, I read Shirley Eder's syndicated review in the Detroit *Free Press.* In this review she admitted that she believed me, even though she was an admirer of my mother.

It was an important admission for this columnist to make in print particularly because the summer before she had written that not too many fans would be interested in this truth.

On the second tour we only did one or two cities a week so that we wouldn't have to leave David Jr. alone very long. But it was every week or every other week that we were on airplanes and in hotels.

There was never a way to tell in advance what kind of reception my book and I would get, so I found myself constantly preparing for the worst. One week a reviewer called the book a bitter and vindictive outrage, the next week another reviewer said she couldn't put the book down because she felt such compassion and a desire to help the young girl in those pages.

What an interesting comment that reading the book was a way of helping the child. Still the tour was a constant rollercoaster ride.

The places all started looking the same to me. All the airports (except perhaps Atlanta), all the hotels, all the food and all the television stations.

Perhaps the process was just becoming more familiar. Perhaps the prescription for Valium my doctor had given me was helping.

We had been on the road constantly for almost five months when David and I left for London to tour England, Scotland and Ireland for the British publishers. It was David's first trip to Europe and I wanted it to be fun for him but I was now near exhaustion from the constant tension.

Durrants Hotel is a quaint, old-fashioned place near Grosvenor Square. It has sort of a Dickensian atmosphere to the tiny rooms and crooked hallways but charming nevertheless. Curiously, I was told many times that Great Britain didn't have a problem with child abuse. So the reporters didn't want to know much about the details, except as it affected the United States. However sensationalistic the British press are reported to be, I had no problem with them. In fact I rather enjoyed hearing their point of view and felt fairly treated by the remarks they printed. I particularly enjoyed meeting a reporter from Northern Ireland who flew down from Belfast to Dublin to interview me at a TV show. It was about 11:30 at night and this man had to return immediately to Belfast. He was still dressed in the battle fatigues worn to cover assignments of bloody street fighting. I felt a kinship. There was no doubt in my mind that he understood. His questions made that clear. He allowed me to ask him questions about the Civil War and the complex reasons behind it. Finding out about the rest of the world fascinated me.

However interesting the people and the tour were, the weather was awful—freezing rain. David caught a cold the third day that persisted until we left. I craved anything chocolate because hot tea wasn't enough to keep me warm.

We experienced a hotel fire at midnight in Manchester and found ourselves on the frozen wet street in our pajamas and raincoats. They had so much snow in Scotland that neither planes or trains could get us into Edinburgh and when we arrived in Dublin, there was a civil-service strike that left garbage everywhere in the streets and no postal service. The crowning glory was a massive march by the PLO that brought the city to a standstill.

Originally the plan was to stay in Dublin a few days, journey out to see the beautiful Irish countryside, then go to Paris before returning to Los Angeles.

None of that plan materialized. Instead, David and I returned to London, back to Durrants Hotel to rearrange our tickets through the British agent. I wanted to go home so badly by now that we booked tickets on the Concorde!

The entire time we were in England the publishers pressured me about going to Australia. I had agreed to go several months earlier, but now it was out of the question. I told Alewyn Birch, managing director of Granada, that I didn't feel well. I'd been on the road six months; I could not get on another plane and travel fourteen hours, it would be the end of me. I was incapable of any more strain and conflict.

I also had the initial symptoms of agoraphobia which was the reason I had this overwhelming need to go home. Neither David nor I understood what was happening to me, with the result that much of my behavior was beginning to appear irrational.

Granada was disappointed with my decision.

Even though I went out of my way to honor every single request they made of me during the English tour and they enjoyed a very successful publication of my book, they remained deeply annoyed.

However, less than three years later, in the fall of 1981, the Queen of England established a new national council to address problems of child abuse and neglect.

PHANTASMAGORIA

PHANTASMAGORIA—n (Gr. *phantasma*, a vision or phantasm; and *agora*, an assembly) Any exhibition of images by means of shadows, as by magic lanterns; especially, such as is produced by a combination of two lanterns by which a gradual change from one set of shadows to another set is effected; hence, any mixed gathering of figures; illusive images.

—WEBSTER'S DICTIONARY,
UNABRIDGED, 1955

I WAS BECOMING very discouraged that Paramount Studios only seemed to want a picture about a 1940s movie star, not what I'd written in my book.

It was the same old sad story. Hollywood changing the content of the book so much that the film only retains the title.

I wrote a second script with more background on the movie star but retained the focus of a mother/daughter relationship as seen from the daughter's viewpoint.

When the day came to deliver it, we sent one copy to the agent and took one copy to Frank Yablans.

David and I met him for breakfast at the Polo Lounge of the Beverly Hills Hotel.

Breakfast was pleasant enough. The usual banter about the studio, the script changes, what I hoped that as the producer he'd help retain in terms of viewpoint and focus.

Then he told us the most amazing story.

As a result of what could be called "independent research" on the historical background of the film and Joan Crawford, Frank said he'd been talking to many different people who knew her in the earlier days.

Among those people was Meyer Lansky, the alleged Jewish Mafia boss of Florida. I just assumed Frank knew him from the *Godfather* films in which Meyer Lansky was portrayed by Lee Strasberg.

In any case, Frank said that in the course of one of his conversations with Meyer Lansky, the picture and Joan Crawford were mentioned. Lansky told Frank that he had always liked "Joanie" and that when she was having so much trouble, he'd helped her get a kid.

"You mean Meyer Lansky helped my mother find a baby to adopt?"

Frank nodded his head in agreement.

"Was it me?"

He nodded again.

I was stunned by this information.

"Guess that could make Meyer Lansky *your* godfather."

I laughed. "Guess so."

My mind careened backwards in time to that newspaper woman I'd met in 1960 while I was doing my first film in Miami. It was she who told me she'd met me when I was just a baby. She said mother had driven across the country with me in May of 1940. We were in Miami on our way to New York where I was to celebrate my first birthday.

I'd previously known about the first birthday in New York. And, I'd known about being adopted in Las Vegas, Nevada, in May 1940. What mother had never mentioned was any trip to Miami in between.

Yet, if Meyer Lansky had been the one who made it possible for her to acquire me as a baby in the first place, then it made a lot more sense why she went to Las Vegas for the adoption procedure and why immediately afterwards she took me to Miami, perhaps to see him, to show her gratitude.

Since the laws of the state of California at that time precluded a single-parent adoption and since she'd been refused as a candidate for adoptive parent by the County of Los Angeles based on personal interviews and assessment of her family relationships, Joan Crawford had a lot to be grateful for to whomever assisted her in her quest for children.

But, it was a strange and unsettling piece of information about my own life, bringing home once again how many parts still were missing in reconstructing the puzzle of my first four years.

No one ever mentioned the second draft of my screenplay again. Despite the fact that the script was on time and contained everything we'd discussed with Yablans, the studio wanted a rewrite. In a November 1, 1978, memo to Frank Yablans from Robert Simpson, I was informed that the first draft followed the book too closely, was too episodic and that no one cared about child abuse.

Paramount continued announcing their purchae of *Mommie Dearest* for feature film production. In print, Frank Yablans was most complimentary to me, commenting to one columnist, "She's a real screenwriter. I'm absolutely astounded by her ability." Next thing we heard, Paramount hired another writer with several more writers to follow in the next year.

Frank Yablans hired five additional writers who created multiple versions of a screenplay for the film. My second draft was never again discussed with me. After it was submitted other writers began work without anyone acknowledging receipt of the material other than to pay me for it.

The next two scripts by other writers were so dreadful that I offered to buy the entire project back from the studio by reimbursing them for every penny they'd spent to date. They refused the offer my lawyer submitted.

The only hopeful element I could see at the time was Anne Bancroft in the title role. I deeply admired her work and felt her performance would add the depth, compassion and strength that the film required.

How she would accomplish it with these scripts was anybody's guess, but there was still time because Yablans couldn't seem to interest a director long enough to sign him.

Yet the book's enormous success in this country in both hardcover and paperback was now well known. It had also been published in England, France, Italy, Japan and Germany.

A companion success was the revolution in public awareness the book had generated over these past three years.

Every newspaper, radio and television station in the country now covered the issue of child abuse as local news on a regular basis. Magazines and journals did special features on the effect, the scope, the treatment. Laws were being changed. A consciousness evolution was occurring at lightning speed, simultaneously across the country.

A door had opened, a path had been cut, a map had been

made. Others followed, millions came forth, voices were being heard. Secrets were being shared. Wounds were beginning to heal. But the legacy of human pain was still everywhere, like slain soldiers on the battlefield. Yet the brave ones continued to come forward and march determinedly.

Personally, I was still considered too controversial to be a guest speaker at ladies' luncheons or be invited to some social gatherings. I learned to accept that as the price of progress. Some of my friends did not.

How, they asked me, visibly upset, can people agree that child abuse is wrong and then say you shouldn't have written the book? How can they separate respect for you from the work you have done to bring this issue into the open public forum?

Everybody in the world was now being mentioned as a potential director for the *Mommie Dearest* film in the press, perhaps in an attempt to keep interest in the project alive. Mike Nichols was approached, as was Franco Zeferelli.

I met Franco at a friend's dinner party in Bel Air while he was currently being touted as a director for *Mommie Dearest.*

It was a fascinating experience because I had long admired his work and was curious to know how he, as a European artist, might envision translating my book into a film.

It was a gay and sparkling dinner, fairly casually given.

When the other guests had left, our hostess Dorothy, David, Franco and I sat around the table talking rather seriously about film in general and this picture in particular.

As Franco talked on about his vision for the film, about creating a vehicle for a great "diva," about his admiration for tragic superstars like Maria Callas and Joan Crawford, my patience wore thin. It was now almost two o'clock in the morning. I was tired. I wanted to go home. Arguing was a pointless, useless process anymore.

I had argued, begged and pleaded with people to read the book, to understand that this was *not* a story about Hollywood, tragic or otherwise. But some still seemed not to listen.

As calmly as possible, feeling the inner fury that had welled up inside me, I told Franco that all the stardom on earth did not excuse irrational, irresponsible adult behavior, particularly to a child. I said that glamor does not give some people more immunity than others from the law or responsibility. To think otherwise is dangerous. As a society we have to care about the innocent, the children. If we cease to care and to demand responsible behavior we are just asking for another Holocaust.

Everyone looked at me as though I'd really stepped over the edge now. I stood up and put on my jacket. David followed me to the front door as I said goodnight to our bewildered hostess.

As David and I stepped out into the chilly early morning air my watch said three o'clock in the morning.

Perhaps it was the hour, perhaps it was the wine or the brandy, perhaps it was my imagination, but I thought I heard a male voice from outside the house say with some urgency—

"But—even Hitler was human!"

I replied, "But I don't care about Hitler—all I care about is how they make this film."

Franco did not direct *Mommie Dearest*. Frank Perry did.

Three years after they'd bought the property, Paramount was finally ready to begin production on the film.

Initially I was pleasantly surprised by the news that Frank Perry would direct. Years ago when my career in theater first began, I was an apprentice at Westport County Playhouse in Connecticut one summer. Frank Perry worked for the Theater Guild in New York, owners of the theater, and he had family living in Westport.

"Big Daddy," as we used to teasingly call him, became my friend. We used to have long talks about getting along with parents, particularly alcoholic parents. We also talked about theater and writing and life in general. Frank was always encouraging to young writers. He lived in Greenwich Village, where I visited him on trips into New York.

So, this was an interesting turn of events. We hadn't seen one another in many years, but certainly Frank knew what the truth was, he must have remembered knowing the truth when he was a part of living through it as my friend.

The film was riddled with setbacks.

One of the most disastrous, the one from which I don't think the production ever recovered, was the loss of Anne Bancroft in the starring role.

David and I were shocked when we heard. Yablans told us that she had script approval, which was standard for a star of her reputation and caliber. He said she didn't give her approval of the final shooting script and that there was apparently no way to resolve the differences.

Anne had been everyone's first choice, mine in particular. For over a year she'd been reading everything she could find about Joan Crawford. She and I had met once and I told her how thrilled I was that she was going to do the part.

Unfortunately, neither David nor I had enough influence with the studio to get her back.

So Anne Bancroft was no longer going to star in the film and the word went out through the Hollywood grapevine like wildfire.

The final script was written by Frank Yablans, Frank Perry, Tracy Hotchner and Robert Gitchell.

It wasn't the worst script in this debacle but it certainly wasn't great, either. It was, however the final one before shooting began.

Since the production was only about a month away from the start date, everyone became a bit frantic about the casting dilemma.

One night, early, Frank Yablans' doorbell rang at home. Evidently no one else was around because Frank himself opened the front door.

The sight that greeted him was a stunning surprise. A shock.

Standing before him was a life-size Joan Crawford!

There she was like a technicolor photo of Crawford, complete with padded shoulders, wearing ankle strap high-heel shoes and a face made up with arched black eyebrows and large blood-red lips.

It was an astonishing resemblance. An apparition. Was it a ghost in real life? No. It was Faye Dunaway!

She had come to Frank's house, costumed and made up to look like Joan Crawford in the 1940s, to convince him she could play the part.

It worked. Faye starred in *Mommie Dearest*.

Diana Scarwid and Mara Hobel were cast to play me at various ages. Both are wonderful actresses and I had high hopes for them.

At the end of the first day of filming, the script supervisor went to the director and told him that if today was any indication, the scenes already shot were running so long that the film would end up being over four hours. The director was not interested.

And so it went. Long scenes, longer waits for the star to

appear from the confines of her trailer ready to work, long delays while the star changed lines of dialog, in effect rewriting the script, scene by scene, day after day.

In the end they had a film over four hours long that could not be edited. So, they fired the first editor.

The second editor solved the problem by cutting out entire sequences, by editing out all the connecting pieces and leaving only highlights. Now, they had a film of normal length, under two hours.

The problem was, the film didn't make any sense. It was like serialized excerpts from a book. Only the sensational material remained and none of the reasons why the behavior took place, exactly as I'd feared all along.

In the initial industry screening, the film got laughs in what were considered the wrong places. The studio was now faced with the real problem of how they were going to market the film.

For my birthday in June, David and I flew to St. Maarten in the Caribbean to stay at a resort on the French side of the island for three or four days.

It was gorgeous. We had a small Mediterranean-style villa right on the ocean with palm trees, long stretches of white-sand beach and blue-green Caribbean ocean within a stone's throw.

But hurricane season had just begun and the small island sweltered. In the beautiful white sand were microscopic creatures like chiggers called "no-seeums" whose bite was bigger than their entire body. In just two days I was covered with vicious red bites, which itched and burned as hot coals dotting my skin.

Before the creatures reached my face, I pleaded with David to get us to New York so that I could recover before my national television appearance with a doctor from

Columbia–Presbyterian Hospital who headed their child-abuse program.

The day was June 12, 1981, just one day after my forty-second birthday.

The hour was a few minutes after 8:00 A.M.

Less than a minute before we were on the air, I was told that they planned to rerun excerpts of an interview with my adopted sister in which she called my book a work of fantasy and me a "person born with evil."

I was dumbfounded. My mind raced but my body was frozen.

The hospital had asked me to come on this program to help child-abuse prevention and their program. This appearance was not for my sake. I had agreed to this appearance to help children who were being abused now.

For the next three minutes after the tape finished, I never stopped talking. I was outraged.

The poor doctor was sitting beside me unable to say a word about his wonderful program.

Some people may have seen this as just one more way to fan fires of controversy in order to promote a Hollywood film, which was due to be released in September, just two or three months later. I saw it differently. To me it was another in a long series of attempts to cheapen and trivialize the facts of violence toward children. By discrediting me, by embroiling me in an unflattering sibling uproar, the focus changed from a serious national epidemic to a trivial personal squabble, which was easier to dismiss than the real issue had proven to be. The continuing insistence by some factions that I had done something wrong by telling the truth about the abuse that had happened to me was in direct opposition not only to the thrust of the federal reporting laws but also to the intent of all the public-service child-abuse-prevention campaigns, which encourage children of all ages to come forward and tell someone if a parent or caretaker is hurting them. I was, at the moment, the only living role model for disclosure that children had. What kind of message was being sent to them and to all the mandated reporters if this was what happened and how one could expect to be treated?

I stormed out of the studio, went back to the Park Lane Hotel and continued to feel outraged. After three years of constant battle, this particular confrontation that I had done nothing to create had the effect of making me feel as though I were being pushed over the edge. I wanted some solutions to the damage that had just been done, not only to me personally but also to the whole issue of protection of children.

What was going on?

While I was trying so hard to behave responsibly according to what I believed was right, why did I always have so much trouble, so much struggle with other people?

How had I tapped into this lethal battle from which I could not seem to exit?

Brought up to think and perform like a man and not like a woman of my generation, I began to realize I had no nurturing. Any mothering in my experience came from women who were paid servants, women who were regularly replaced.

I didn't have a childhood. I had an upbringing.

Now, I had no healthy experience of parental caring to recall in my time of need, no recollection of sustained love to steer my course in these turbulent waters. My life was not equipped with radar to warn me of impending collision. I had no built-in sensors to guide me away from disaster.

So my course continued, fueled by anger, by outrage,

propelled by the belief that once on this track, I had no other choice.

So when this present process finally unearthed the profound real feelings inside me, I realized that there had been a great and deep sadness, a fundamental disappointment about my life, a wounded quality to all the events that had happened to me. It was this sense of being deeply wounded that colored the outlook, the perspective, the evolution of how all the years fit together.

And time was when the sadness comprised everything: the profound sadness, beyond any outside view, the sadness running through blood in the heart, behind tears in the eyes, even permeating the air that breathed life into my body.

It is a lonely sadness, not a weeping or crying sadness such as one that visits when death is present.

There are few tears with this sadness, as though to begin the grieving process would signal the end of this life. The sadness is now too long, too great, too deep. Crying would only acknowledge the hopeless impossibility of getting rid of that sadness. Crying would not help solve anything for me, yet.

My life was raw to the bone, skin seared away by controversy, flesh inflamed by injustice. My body burned in the torment of rage. It was consumed daily. There was now no rest, no peace, no respite, no solace.

Life was total war. My body was the point of the arrow dipped in blood. The warrior's spear, the hunter's arrow. My life was the point of the arrow dipped in blood, my own blood, dipped in a raging white heat of boiling blood.

The values I'd been taught to live by...the skills the world gave me...the fighting, the chaos, terror and aggressiveness...were killing me. There was no love. No nurturing. Wisdom, justice, kindness did not exist.

What the world was teaching me was that my exposure of child abuse, as unacceptable behavior, was in direct conflict with social values that rank power, control, and repression of children and women very high. The exposure of child abuse in millions of homes became a direct threat to the established order of parenting and therefore of acceptable social control through violence, whenever necessary. People were caught in a trap between being afraid of what their own children would say about them and what they believed about their own parents' behavior toward them now that the words were available to think about the past in different terms, in a different light.

Ridicule of me was a way of desensitizing the issue, a way of reframing the issue, of renaming it, by trivializing it so as to prevent the power of this revelation from becoming a legitimate social force.

This issue relates to violence as a means of all social control from the time of early childhood and it directly attacked the predominant social order of repressive domination throughout five thousand years of history. It was an uprising of the least, the weakest, the most disenfranchised of all segments of humanity. It was an uprising of the CHILDREN!

Minorities and women had technically been set free, but their children were still enslaved, their minds and hearts poisoned by acts of uncontrolled brutality and sustained torture.

All of this was sanctioned by society in the name of "parenting." It is here, in the systematic terrorizing atmosphere we call childhood, that the values of our world are taught and the unmasking of barbaric behavior unveiled.

The depths of the torture, the far reaches of the barbarism seething beneath the surface of everyday life is horrifying when it periodically gushes into view through vicious acts of prolonged, premeditated cruelty such as serial rapes, mass murderers, satanic cults using children as human sacrifice under the banner of religion. Is it any wonder that we have anarchy in our city streets? Is it any wonder that we are so far removed from a world of peaceful coexistence? Is it any wonder that stress and drugs are creating chaos and killing us?

Unfortunately, these acts are still a measure of how deeply ingrained the myths of rule by force, control by dominance, management by repressive power still are in our world today.

The fact that we're able to see it at all is a mark of progress. Someday, regular childhood histories will be required by police departments in cases of homicide, rape, cult and drug offenders. Then this evidence will make it clear that what happened in the offender's own childhood is now being brutally played out against society.

Earlier, we couldn't recognize the problem because we couldn't see through the present social structure to understand the cruelty. The social structure itself was still too cruel and unfair to a vast number of citizens (blacks, women, Indians, the poor, the immigrants, the elderly, the sick, the children, the animals and the very earth herself), to be evaluated from any alternative perspective. We needed to live through the ecology and peace movements, the liberation of women and minorities before we could begin to address the issues concerning the children of all.

In 1981, I knew I was in the forefront of this journey of liberation. I also knew that the process was killing me.

This is the silver-haired, green-eyed child I found lost among the ruins of my past.

With Mommie Dearest when I was a baby, 1940.

My first birthday, in New York City, after visit to Miami and Las Vegas for adoption arranged, I later learned, by Meyer Lansky.

James MacArthur watches over me at the Nyack, New York, home of his mother, Helen Hayes.

Mother and I in the garden of the Brentwood, California, home where I grew up.

Mother with brother
Chris and me at the
Pebble Beach Lodge
in Carmel, California,
in 1946.

Here I am protecting
Chris wrapped in step-
father Phillip Terry's
coat at Carmel Beach
in 1946.

The photograph of Mommie Dearest and me used on the jacket of my first book.

At the age of 12, I am still being dressed in "mother and daughter" dresses.

After graduating from high school, I had to make my way in the world. Here, in New York, 1958, working as a photographer's model. I am 19 years old.

The National Company of *Barefoot in the Park,* from left, Sandor Szabo, Philip Clark, Myrna Loy, and myself.

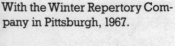

With the Winter Repertory Company in Pittsburgh, 1967.

Again working as a photographer's model in New York City, 1969.

With my mother, working at a charity telethon in New York City in 1969.

Right: Dressed for a Chevy Truck commercial shot in Los Angeles in 1972. On this job I met my future husband, David Koontz, when he hired me to do some stunt driving.

On vacation in Mazatlan, Mexico, in 1972.

At Marina del Rey, with David during our courtship, and his son, age 10, in 1973.

Our wedding day, February 14, 1976, in Palos Verdes, California.

Publicity photograph for
Mommie Dearest, 1978.
(CREDIT: TOM BERT)

At the Tower of London during a break on tour for the British edition of *Mommie Dearest,* April, 1979. I was exhausted during this trip, but here, it doesn't show.

Ad for the movie *Mommie Dearest*, starring Faye Dunaway as Joan Crawford.

Photograph taken when I first arrived home from the hospital after recovering from my stroke, August, 1981. My hair had been cropped before and after surgery.

With David for support on Santa Monica beach, September, 1981.

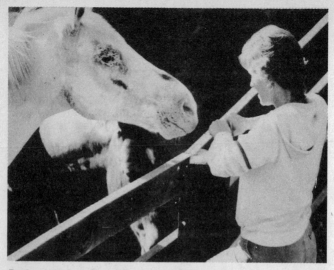

At the ranch in San Luis Obispo, I could relax and I discovered I had to change my way of being in the world. Here, with Pappy, my big, stubborn "Appy" in 1982.

Talking to Pepper at the ranch, 1982.

With David at the ranch near one of the lakes, 1984. This is one of the last photos of us together.
(CREDIT: ROBERT LAWRENCE BALSER)

Mother, Chris and I in a family publicity photo, autographed to stepfather Phillip Terry, in mother's handwriting. I am 6 years old, my brother about 3 years old.

Phillip, mother and I, age 4, in the library. Phillip was the only one of mother's husbands who took any interest in me and whom I considered a father.

One day my stepfather disappeared from my life, with Mother offering no explanation. Here, his hands and feet remain in a photo of me at my birthday party, but the rest of his image was ripped out of my scrapbook when my parents divorced.

Phillip tried to reestablish contact with me, as here in Santa Barbara in 1980, but I had trouble trusting him even after Mother died.

With Phillip in 1987, after each of us had recovered from our strokes and I was able to accept his attempts at reconnection.
(CREDIT: BEVERLY JACKSON)

Public speaking in Dallas, 1983.

With Governor Jim Thompson of Illinois at opening of statewide child abuse hotline, 1985.

With fellow Commissioner Tom Beckett and Los Angeles County Supervisor Deane Dana at opening of family waiting room in Children's Dependency Court, 1987.

PART TWO

LOST IS A PLACE, TOO

LONE SOLDIER

AN ETERNITY HAS passed. A life has come and gone. The surreal mirage of a masked and gowned nurse looms over me. Shadows ebb and flow as though seen through water, as visions seen through closed eyes. The air is cold. Slowly my eyes open. The light is a steady pale brightness. The face of the mirage moves. It is a real face. A human face. The masked face has real eyes. Then I hear a soft, faraway sound. The eyes of the nurse peer closely. She recognizes the noise as a sound from me. I have a voice! Oh—my goodness . . . perhaps I am alive!

The next time I opened my eyes, I saw Dr. Heifetz standing before me. He asked me questions in rapid succession: What day was it? What year? When had I been born? How old was I? Where was I now? How many fingers had he held up?

I couldn't speak words but made some sounds indicating a glimmer of recognition.

Suddenly he was quiet, his eyes searching my face. I waited. Very gently he touched my arm.

"Rest, I'll see you later."

In the hallway, David sat nervously waiting.

Dr. Heifetz appeared.

"You can go in and see her," Dr. Heifetz said.

David went straight to the recovery room. He touched my face as I was just coming out of the anesthesia. Two nurses hovered. He held my hand.

David leaned down close over the plastic cup that covered my nose and mouth and listened to the hiss of my breath, in and out. He saw my eyes flutter. David looked closely at my bare face and head covered with iodine. The hair had been shaved off the left side of my head for the operation and there was a huge bandage covering the portion of my head where they had cut the skull open. I was hooked up to all sorts of monitoring devices in this space-age intensive care room.

As David leaned down he whispered:

"My darling, you made it, my baby, you made it, I'm so proud of you... God, I love you." He swallowed back tears. "You did, you beat it."

He smiled back at me as he saw that I smiled faintly and then I closed my eyes.

"I love you so much, just keep comin' baby, just keep comin'." Then he stepped away from the bed.

I was still gradually coming out of the anesthesia and the nurse asked my name. Although I couldn't talk, I made sounds and acknowledged by nodding slightly or moving my left hand.

David thought, my God, she's stronger... she's better than I am. If that nurse had asked me those same questions right now, I couldn't have told her where I lived; I couldn't have told her my name. I couldn't have told her anything. Thank you, God, she's gonna do it.

Three minutes passed, then four, and then five. I had made that next five minutes.

I opened my eyes again and saw my beloved husband's face. I had the feeling that he was consciously willing me to stay alive. David believed that I would live. I had prayed to God to let me live. I sensed that the strange journey I had just been through wasn't over yet.

David went back to see everybody in the waiting area. That's when it hit him. He excused himself, went down the hall toward the telephone, and wept. "Oh, God, please help her, please don't desert her ... please, oh God." Alone he screamed his pain and it all came out. The four days of terror was out—the four days of agony. He had never imagined there could be such pain. No one who had seen me the Sunday before riding the beautiful horse with my blond hair blowing in the wind, could have imagined my rapid decline to the creature whose head was half-shaved, whose hair and face were splotched with iodine, who was barely breathing through the use of oxygen, coupled to machines with wires.

The next room in which I awakened was perpetually dark, another space-age module in the intensive care unit of the hospital. Someone was always with me when I opened my eyes. I barely moved, my body was so weak. I realized that I was electronically wired to monitoring systems. I saw the intravenous tubes. At frequent intervals, the nurse gave me water to drink through a straw.

David was only allowed to visit for a few minutes each hour. Yet his face is emblazoned upon my memory forever. He was everything that had made my life wonderful. I adored him. Now I was completely dependent on him to interpret the world for me. The moments I saw him were my only sense of continuity in ever-present darkness.

Very quietly the nurse would say to David, "You can come back in a while."

Though it was midnight, David told me later the lobby seemed to be filled with friends. David greeted each one, knowing he couldn't have made it without them. He gathered strength from them. He was nearing exhaustion. His mother and friends stood by encouragingly as he took their love in an attempt to transfer it back to me.

He confided to someone later, "I would go back in and I would tell her how much I love her and touch her face, be with her, pray beside her. I would smile and try always to be happy, try to let her know how happy I was that she was doing so well, and that I was so proud of her. I never could let her know how worried I was. I would go out of the room, I would gather my strength and come back."

Throughout that nightmarish time, David would always remember to call his son with updates. "She's getting stronger as each four-minute period passed," he would assure David Jr.

David Jr. had just started his first year of college at Cal Poly in San Luis Obispo and was living in the dorms, taking these calls on a friend's phone. These communications became a source of strength both for father and son.

On Thursday, August 6, David was in the room at about 2:30 in the morning when I finally fell asleep. He could now tell that my condition was stable. Strange, he thought, to become so familiar with all of the various electronic life-support systems' monitors.

At almost three o'clock in the morning, he left but was

back at six o'clock. He simply sat in the lobby maintaining his vigil.

Hearing someone approach, David looked up and saw the doctor for the first time since the night before.

"I was just with her," Dr. Heifetz said, "and I believe in miracles...God does not want her to go away. Just keep your fingers crossed now, hour by hour...there's no guarantee that something can't go wrong. We'll know more by the end of the day. Just keep praying, and don't give up hope." He smiled warmly.

As the morning wore on, our friends began arriving. David would tell me of all of the people in the lobby who were sending me their love and support, trying to boost my spirits. I was actually starting to smile, and could begin to say a few sounds now. The sounds were disconnected but stronger than they had been, so David felt I was beginning to get a new blood supply to my brain.

Then it dawned on David what the doctor really had said. What he knew and I didn't, was that now the concern was with the fact that the big clot, which was still in the carotid artery, could break loose, shooting a piece up into my brain, causing massive hemorrhaging. All would be lost. It was a matter of time; the longer nothing happened, the better chance I had.

David pleaded with the doctor to let him know what to expect. "How long, how long, doctor, do we have to wait... three, four weeks...oh my God, this is like playing Russian roulette."

The doctor replied, "Now, David, I don't want you to be concerned about that. The only thing I want you to be concerned about is that the recuperation is coming along and that she's getting better, and that the blood supply seems to be coming."

* * *

On Friday, August 7, late in the afternoon, the nurses began preparing me to leave the intensive care unit. Slowly and carefully they began unattaching me from the monitoring sensors and finally from the intravenous. I was being transferred to a room on the eighth floor, where my husband was waiting. I still felt extremely weak, but the transfer definitely meant that I was making good progress.

Leaving the quiet dimness of intensive care was a shock to my senses. All of a sudden there were sounds and colors surrounding me, bombarding my eyes and ears. Although I was still in the hospital, I was back among the living.

My new room on the eighth floor was directly across from the nurses' station. Two nurses helped the gurney attendants transfer me into my waiting bed. For the first time I realized that I had a wide surgical collar around my neck. Everyone handled me with great care.

David smiled and held my left hand. It seemed to me that he had been with me every single moment since Monday, either in person or in spirit. There were beautiful flowers already in the room and more arrived. They were a sea of color filling the air with fragrance. I was very tired but looking forward to my first meal.

That night David insisted on sleeping at the hospital on the couch in my room near my bed. I was overjoyed at the prospect of being with him once again but worried that he'd wake up with a terrible crick in his neck. Since I couldn't communicate any of my worries, I just smiled gratefully.

Saturday was my first visiting day. I was allowed to have visitors for a total of three minutes each hour. I was overwhelmed. Many of the women I worked with on the charity organization board spent the whole day at the hospital with my David. I felt enormously loved, more so than at any other time in my life. I could barely move, I could only speak a few halting words, and yet we were able to communicate. Strange that so many good feelings of love and caring filled a time of such tragedy.

David had to help me eat. My left hand was not skilled enough, though I was carefully trying to learn to negotiate with it. My right hand and arm were useless, completely paralyzed, without feeling or motion. In fact I had to learn to pay very careful attention to positioning myself, always looking to see where my right hand was located, so that I wouldn't inadvertently hurt myself. It is a very strange feeling having a living appendage to your body that has no feeling. It is not something you get used to easily.

I had partial paralysis on the right side of my face. It was considered minor and didn't significantly distort my features. However, I soon discovered that eating could be extremely hazardous. Since the right side of my mouth also had no feeling, I couldn't tell when pieces of food were stuck between my gum and cheek. As with a chipmunk, pockets of food built up that could cause sudden choking. I also had to learn to eat small spoonfuls very slowly because the entire involuntary chewing/swallowing responses had been disrupted.

Many times during the first few days David actually had to reach his fingers inside my mouth—exactly as one might do with a baby—and dislodge food so that I wouldn't choke.

Nobody told me to expect this level of complete helplessness. I was deeply embarrassed. Humiliated, I couldn't even use words to ask for help. I had to point and open my mouth like a baby bird. My husband was the essence of patience and compassion. Somehow he never showed me his fear, but appeared calm and resourceful.

The nurse helped me to walk very slowly to the bathroom

that night. It was then that I saw myself in the mirror for the first time since the past Monday, when I had left home in the ambulance. What looked back at me from the mirror was an apparition...a freak...a zombie...a total stranger.

My knees buckled in shock. I steadied myself with my left hand, mustered my courage and stared intently at the zombie creature appearing before me in the bathroom mirror. One half of my head was shaved and partially covered with a bandage. The other half of my shoulder-length blond hair was horribly tangled, matted, and splotched with dark reddish brown surgical iodine. The skin color of my face was ashen. The normally green eyes had turned to pale hazel. As I looked further down my body I saw that the back of my right hand was blackened from an intravenous needle hemorrhage. Both arms were badly bruised from intravenous injections. The angiogram test had left a huge, ugly black bruise on my right leg at the groin. This leg bruise covered the inside of my thigh, halfway to the knee.

In horror I stared at myself in the mirror, wondering how I was ever going to get to know this total stranger who was supposed to be me. I looked like the lone surviving soldier of fierce combat on a battlefield I barely remembered. But, judging from the extent of my wounds, it had been a hell of a war.

I had never been a person who was comfortable with hospitals or at the sight of blood. I had never been good at nursing anyone, even myself. So my reaction to this horrifying silent confrontation with the sight of my body in the mirror was not typical of me in the least. Instead, I was very calm. I simply stared dispassionately at the extensive physical damage in the human image I saw. Perhaps, like that lone surviving soldier, I had been totally desensitized by what had happened to me during the preceding week of battle. Curiously, I remembered only that there had been emotional agony but surprisingly little physical pain except for the angiogram.

My personal experience of my own near-death had been a relentlessness. Not a sense of intense physical danger, but rather a terrifying reduction of all life forces, a decline in all means of human communication, a loss of all the faculties that distinguish me as a human being. The sense of violence I had experienced had been more closely related to starvation or suffocation or freezing to death than to physical pain. Yet I knew that it was a miracle that I was alive at all.

After seeing myself in the mirror and using a sort of sign language to communicate my distress, David arranged for the rest of my hair to be cut off. With half my head shaved and bandaged while the other half was matted and iodine-splotched hair, I resembled a creature out of the *Marat/Sade* drama—an inmate of the medieval asylum called Bedlam. We both agreed that having my head shaved and being temporarily bald would definitely be a preferable alternative. But, it was a condition that would be quite an adjustment!

The total removal of my physical, mental and psychological vanities was only one of the many unexpected events in this strange process of personal catastrophe. Everything I had been previously proud to possess was taken away from me. Yet, at the moment, I had no particularly strong feelings about any of it. Curiously again, I simply took note of each major difference between the past and present "me," then tried to fit the new information into the puzzle of this altered self.

I was now able to move into a chair for part of the morning and afternoon. The chair was where I ate my meals. Surrounded by beautiful flowers and plants, I could imagine I was sitting in a garden rather than in a hospital room.

Every hour I was allowed a few visitors. So many loving faces...so many gestures of caring. I remember seeing a number of people each day. But I tired very easily, and trying to talk was exhausting. Everyone seemed to understand that they could only stay a few moments. The day went quickly. David had brought my Bible and although I couldn't read, I stared at the Psalms. When I was alone or when I became too tired, I just held onto the Bible and prayed without being able to say any words aloud.

David never left me for more than an hour. He managed to be cheerful the entire time. I was virtually helpless, though now somewhat ambulatory. On Sunday evening, David went home to sleep for the first time.

CHILD'S PLAY

BRIGHT AND EARLY Monday morning after breakfast, the speech therapist arrived. David introduced himself to her and then left us alone for my first lesson.

I didn't know exactly what to expect. The woman had a smile on her face and some books in her hand that appeared to be for children. When she opened the brightly colored book to the first page I saw pictures and large letters. She smiled and asked me if I would like to read the top sentence.

Suddenly it dawned on me. My heart sank like a stone being thrown from a high-rise building. Something awful was wrong. It was an ominous realization. Something else had happened to me. The innocent-looking children's book sitting on the table in front of me was too difficult for me to understand! I was unable to tell the therapist what the pictures meant exactly, nor could I make out most of the words. I blinked my eyes several times, trying to keep from crying. I knew this was a book for beginning readers, for five-year-old children. I, who had a master's degree in communication, could not understand this children's primer. A feeling of humiliation welled up in my throat and flushed across my face. Swallowing hard, I attempted to pronounce the first words. Stumbling and halting, I barely got through to the end.

She read along with me, which made this time of torturous reality go faster. She corrected all the mistakes as we went. I was being transported in an invisible time machine, taken back in my feelings to what it was like to be a child in kindergarten or first grade.

Educational skills that had come totally without conscious thought just one week ago now took the same work as when a child learns them for the first time. Except, there was no reward because all I could think of was the loss of my previous ability, that this was another skill I *used* to have. Now, I had to sound out all the syllables and was still mystified by the meanings of the sounds that these made words.

But, I was not five or six years old. I was a woman of forty-two. In an attempt to explain the situation to me they told me I had aphasia. Aphasia: the technical term for the loss of your power of speech and/or the ability to use words appropriately, due to disease or injury of the brain. Major aphasia is loss of control of the muscles used in speech. Sensory aphasia is a loss of memory for words. I had some of both kinds of aphasia due to my stroke and subsequent brain damage.

That same day the physical therapist made her initial visit. Her work was more fun. With her strong arm around my waist, holding and guiding me, we walked around my room and then several yards down the hallway. I realized that my body didn't move naturally. My arms and legs were not coordinated. She had to teach me to alternate my arm movements swinging first the left and then the right rather than allowing my right arm to just hang limply by my side as I tried to walk. I felt like a tin soldier mechanically marching at a halting snail's pace. Actually, I felt like a total fool.

Everyone said I was doing very well, so I tried to feel good about my first active day. I was very tired.

David reminded me that the football game, which I loved watching, was on that night. Late that afternoon two of our friends came by the hospital with a big surprise for me.

They trouped into the room carrying an official Los Angeles Rams lap robe and numbered football jersey. And, as if that weren't enough, they also produced a huge bowl of popcorn and two cans of beer. Then they turned on the television set to "Monday Night Football" and bundled me up in the blue-and-gold lap robe. Even the nurses got a good laugh out of the antics. David took the food and beer home but I kept the lap robe and jersey.

While I watched the game, our delightful, crazy friends took David out to dinner.

The next day, Tuesday, both the speech and physical therapists visited me again. Concentrating on what they tried to help me learn was very hard work for me. Neither my mind nor my body seemed easily managed. By the end of each half-hour session, I was ready to go back to bed, exhausted.

Dr. Heifetz also visited that day. He changed the bandage on my head for a smaller one and then told me to walk for him.

I thought I was doing pretty well, shuffling slowly and carefully from chair to bed.

But that progress was not what the doctor had in mind. I was dressed only in a hospital gown, open in the back, but Dr. Heifetz paid no attention to my scanty attire.

"Don't act like an old lady," he said very firmly. "I want

you to hold your head up, straighten your back out, and Walk-Walk-Walk!"

Holding on to me by the neck of my hospital gown, the doctor literally propelled me out the door of my room and into the hallway, heading for the nurses' station.

I was so astonished, I didn't have time to be embarrassed about the peculiar costume for my public hallway appearance. I simply did what the doctor told me to do as best I could. After all, this was the man who had saved my life. I never even thought to question him.

As it turned out, I could indeed walk far better than I thought I could. My husband, however, was about to faint with anxiety and fear that I'd fall and hurt myself. What David couldn't know was that the doctor had an iron grip on me and I knew I was safe, if slightly under-dressed for the occasion.

The doctor had proved a very important point to me. The real lesson of this unorthodox experience was that I was going to have to push myself to the limit and even beyond in order to regain the mental and physical capabilities that I had taken for granted just ten days earlier. It was not good for me to sit like a lump and let things be done for me. He put me on notice that the retraining of my mind and body were about to begin with seriousness.

There is a tendency I discovered first in myself, and later in others, to think of a stroke as resembling a heart attack or a serious case of flu in terms of recovery. It's as though you know you're sick, but when the operation is successfully over or the virus subsides...you assume you are going to be restored to the same person you were before. I found myself waking up each morning expecting to stretch my right arm and find that it had returned to normal. It didn't. There were other days when I woke up fully expecting to resume talking in full sentences with all the words in their proper places. I couldn't.

I wanted to get well and go home so badly that I worked hard at everything, yet I still had to face the possibility that I might never be able to completely care for myself, never be able to go back to work or rejoin normal people as an equal again. Of course, there was always hope, but no one would or could yet predict what the future held for me. Everyone told me it was quite enough progress right now just to be alive.

David went home every night to sleep but he was with me from early morning until nine or ten o'clock at night. At mealtimes he cut up all my food into little pieces. I was sometimes able to feed myself with my left hand, but if I couldn't he helped me. He encouraged me every two hours to do the exercises they had taught me to help strengthen my right hand. He took me for walks down the hall. He loved me and stood by me every single waking moment of this time in the hospital. It was my husband who noticed subtle changes in my daily progress and told me that I was improving.

On Wednesday afternoon, one week after my brain operation, two members of the staff at Schulman Rehabilitation Center came to visit me. I had been told that if they accepted my application I would be transferred there on Friday. Schulman was a separate rehabilitation facility that was connected with the hospital. It had rather strict standards. I had already been told that I was on the borderline of qualifying for acceptance because I was ambulatory and most patients were restricted to wheelchairs.

California had what I thought were very strange regulations for admittance to rehabilitation hospitals. It seemed that patients were disqualified if they could *walk*, no matter what other serious problems they had. It was true that I could manage to walk with assistance, but the rest of my right side was paralyzed. I could barely talk, could not care for myself, and my mind was impaired by brain damage. I couldn't figure out what in the world my feet working had to do with my mouth and brain *not* working and why that might prevent me from meeting admission qualifications!

Schulman would be my transition between hospital and home. I did have serious speech problems and physical paralysis, which were going to need extended therapy. No one had told me how long I'd be in Schulman if they accepted me.

The interview went well. I felt that I'd like the people at Schulman if I was sent there. They explained the program in detail. Every day I would have six hours of speech, occupational and physical therapy. The speech therapy would help me not only to learn to talk properly but also to retrain my brain to think logically and deal with numbers as well as letters. The occupational therapy would teach me how to care for myself outside the hospital setting and strengthen my eye/hand coordination. The physical therapy would be like a gym class involving body coordination, muscle strengthening, and increased stamina.

At Schulman, meals would be served at large tables in a group dining room that all patients shared. Visiting hours would be after five in the evening, on Saturday afternoon, and all day Sunday. Their only patient under fifty was a man of thirty-five. The head nurse asked if I would find that depressing. I told her I didn't think so. The interview ended, and soon afterward I was told my application had been accepted.

As the hurricane aspect of my stroke subsided, David watched the friends who had been so very helpful, loving, and supportive during the height of the disaster gradually return to the normalcy of their own lives. The waiting room was now empty. David suddenly felt very alone.

During these days David often walked back through the larger waiting room, where he had sat outside the operating room. Now he watched other groups, other families huddled in terror as they waited for the results from the doctors coming out to inform them of the status of their loved ones.

He thought, Lord, I know how you feel. I'm sorry. Then looking up, he would say "Thank you, God, for letting her live."

Then David would reflect on how ironic it was that during this same period of time the film of *Mommie Dearest* was opening nationwide, under Paramount's marketing efforts, to mixed reviews. David thought it was bizarre that there was a movie playing in theaters all over the United States about my life while I was in the hospital having just narrowly escaped death. What he couldn't know was that, because we didn't want a lot of publicity about my illness and brain operation, rumors were spreading in the show business community that I'd had a nervous breakdown and had been hospitalized for that condition rather than the stroke.

SUNDAY LAUGHTER

THE SCHULMAN CENTER was the original part of the hospital. Patients were housed on the top floor. Speech and occupational therapy were located on the second floor and the physical therapy gym was on the ground floor near the entrance.

My room was plain but pleasant with a view of the Hollywood hills. The head nurse and social worker were on hand to greet us upon my arrival. They explained the daily routine and then left me to settle into my new surroundings.

Today there were no activities, no visitors, just me, sitting by myself in a wheelchair I didn't know how to operate.

I felt a sense of sadness well up in me. Maybe it was self-pity. Maybe it was also anxiety. I looked around the room, wondering what I should do to keep myself busy.

It was then I spotted the coloring book and a set of pens on the bedside table. How clever a gift. I thought that learning to hold the felt-tipped colored pens was exactly the exercise I needed if I was going to learn how to write again but it would have been a very boring experience without the coloring book. The large pens were relatively easy to hold and the tip required almost no pressure. As I still had no sense of pressure or grip strength in my right hand, these gifts were part of the perfect tools to use in skill recovery.

I settled myself down, took a deep breath, and opened to a page containing a single Persian cat.

Figuring out how to open the box of colored pens was more difficult. The box had a sliding lid, which would normally require two hands. I held the box between my knees and pushed the lid with my left hand. After several unsuccessful attempts, I watched the box open finally with a sense of triumph.

In the past, hundreds of ordinary little things tasks had been taken for granted. Now they required a lot of effort and ingenuity. I saw that they would be a source of continuing frustration, but I also realized that sometimes my efforts would bring some measure of success.

The next step was to hold the pen in my right hand and learn to guide it along the lines of the picture. I could use my hand only if I looked directly at what I was doing and concentrated the entire time. If I shifted my attention, even briefly, whatever object I had in my hand would drop to the floor. The practice of holding the long coloring pen would help me to relearn how to use a fork, brush my teeth, write my name and generally strengthen the muscles that had not been used since my stroke almost two weeks before and with which my brain had apparently lost normal communications.

While I was struggling against feelings of loneliness, fear, and the nasty twinges of self-pity, an old man appeared in the doorway, smiling at me. His introduction was casual, telling me his name, that he was a volunteer, and that he was over eighty years old. I stared at him in astonishment. I had not heard him appear. He was nicely dressed, had a wonderful shock of white hair, and wore a hearing aid. Since I could barely talk he generated the entire conversation.

"Can I see your picture?" he asked kindly.

I smiled, turning the coloring book around. My cat was composed of crazy colors with a bright crimson face, green fur and brown legs.

He said, "Cats are not my favorites." I decided that my picture probably hadn't helped.

"Is there anything I can do for you or get for you?"

I pointed to the ginger ale can and gestured for him to open it for me. As he talked with me, I felt better. He had great dignity and kindness, which he managed to impart to me without making me feel beholden or invalid. At eighty, he was also justifiably proud of being able to help others. I marveled at his attitude and Good Samaritan spirit. He had helped me feel welcome and less alone by taking the time to give me the benefit of his own humanity.

On Sunday, breakfast was served later than usual. On the TV set I watched a Jimmy Swaggart religious program with thundering, foot-thumping gospel music as I waited for the nurse. It was then I realized that being so close to death had not necessarily put me in touch with God. What I had experienced in the past two weeks had provided me with first-hand knowledge of the fleeting quality of my life and had kindled the need for a deep renewal of my faith. How thin and fragile a thread held me between life and death. How precious life was and how little I had understood the true joy of just being alive.

The joy itself is a gift. Life is a gift—and not just in the measurement of success or accomplishment. Too often the quality of each day is spent subverted to some distant dream. In pursuit of the spectacular, we waste our lives. We neglect today because we're blaming the past or are fantasizing about the future. But I now know that today is all I have.

Perhaps because the normal routine had been broken, I sensed anxiety in the dining room when my nurse wheeled me into place at the round table. Many patients were awaiting the weekly visits of their entire families. Other people knew there would be no one to see them. One woman was celebrating her birthday and her husband had planned a party for her that afternoon.

I sat in my wheelchair pulled up to a table with three other women who were also in wheelchairs. At the next table were two women who were chronically ill in addition to their physical disability and at a third table were five men. One of the men was always cheerful. Some of the others complained a lot. At a fourth table a younger man sat alone because he couldn't get along with anyone.

There was also a rather extraordinary woman almost ninety years old, who was convinced that there was a conspiracy against her among the nurses. She was very independent. She was determined to get out of the hospital and do so by walking off the ward. She kept trying to get out of her wheelchair, causing the nurses constant stress, while in danger of giving herself a concussion or broken hip in her escape attempts. After the second time, when she caused the wheelchair to tip over, pinning her underneath, the nurses had no choice but to construct a harness that secured her to the wheelchair.

This Sunday morning the woman was most distraught. Wiggle and twist as she might, she couldn't untie herself. Unlike the majority of us who were stroke victims and unable to speak fluently, this woman talked a blue streak. She refused to eat, insisted that someone call her family, and implored all of us other patients to come to her assistance when the nurses were out of the room.

There was something quite hilarious and crazy about this drama. It had all the elements necessary for the black humor that develops out of tragic situations and is always just around the corner in hospitals or institutions. Such humor is really the saving grace of disasters. Not one person in the room could talk normally or walk without assistance. The cheerful man told the old woman to stop complaining because she'd brought the situation on herself. If she hadn't purposely fallen out of the wheelchair just to get attention, the nurses wouldn't have had to harness her. The old woman didn't like that remark and renewed her pleas.

"Somebody help me! Somebody help me!" she demanded loudly, looking frantically around at each of us.

All eyes in the room were focused on her. A woman at my table who had a good sense of humor and could talk better than the rest of us chimed in, "My dear, you're asking for help from the wrong group!"

Everyone in the dining room laughed out loud, except the old lady. As we looked around at one another, we were struck by how ludicrous it was that she was asking *us* for help. None of us could help ourselves, never mind someone else.

It was the first time I had actually laughed at my own disability. It may have caused the old woman some discomfort, but it was good for the rest of us. Not so very long before, each one of the patients in the room had been a functioning person, responsible for families and businesses. Now each of us was helpless, frustrated in our efforts to learn, and periodically embarrassed that we made such a mess of the everyday tasks of taking care of ourselves.

In that moment of laughter we put aside the disappointments and gained a valuable new perspective on our own lives. After that incident, I noticed myself being more kind and open with fellow patients. I even tried to talk to the young man who was so openly hostile and thought no one liked him. I encouraged the darling Jewish lady at my table who worked so hard on the exercise to touch her fingers together and I listened empathetically to a woman who'd been married fifty-four years and was deeply worried about how her husband was getting along without her at home. The fabric of gentle kindness made all our lives better. We were now more able to share our struggles with the therapy and the fears each of us had about what would happen when we went home.

The only person who was not positively affected by the laughter and sharing that Sunday morning was the old lady. After breakfast that morning the nurses put her back to bed. In her room, while she waited for her family to arrive, the woman took the false teeth out of her mouth and beat the dentures on the bed table while screaming over and over again at the top of her lungs, "Help me . . . someone please help me."

COMING HOME

ON THE DAY I returned home, my heart was overflowing with sheer joy. To see the familiar neighborhood streets again, to see scarlet blossoms covering the crepe myrtle trees in the sweltering desert heat of August, was astonishing. As the ambulance approached our driveway, I heard the dogs barking. So many times in the past their shrill yapping had annoyed me but today they were transformed into the homecoming cheering section.

There was a huge bouquet of flowers with a pink "Welcome Home" banner waiting on the hall table. *Home.* I never thought I'd see it again. Tears streamed down my face.

For the first few days my schedule at home closely resembled the hospital routine. My nurse would arrive at eight in the morning and help me bathe. It was much too dangerous for me to attempt to manage the shower alone. The combination of water and soap posed an imminent threat of falling. I still wore a large, heavy neck brace, which was carefully removed when I washed, but I was cautioned to be careful of any quick movement.

My body had little stamina. Just the exertion of bathing and dressing would require a brief rest. The occupational therapist in the hospital had already taught me how to dress myself, using my functional left hand, and after that task was accomplished and I had rested, Nurse and I would be off for our walk.

The summer temperature in the San Fernando Valley could easily reach 100 degrees by noon. I was as white as a sheet and as bald as an old man. Wearing a very large sun hat and accompanied by my nurse, I must have created quite a sight for passersby. The first day I was only able to walk one short block. Each subsequent day we tried walking a little bit further.

There is a rhythm to walking that I had never noticed before the stroke. Anyone who has experienced military training is aware that the sequence of arm-swinging and step-taking is important and does not necessarily "come naturally." At this point I still walked like a tin soldier—out of step.

A large part of the problem was that I didn't have much feeling in my entire right side. I had to think about every single movement, like a dancer learning combinations of new dance steps to form a pattern. I could feel that my arms and legs were moving, but I did not know much about the finesse with which they were performing the actions. It was an experiment in new self-perception.

I believed that God had spared my life for a purpose. Even though that purpose was beyond my understanding at this time, I was going to do my best to recover completely.

Because my right hand was as yet unable to function, I learned to use my left hand to perform most ordinary tasks.

Eating, however, was a daily trial. It was an embarrassing and exhausting ordeal. The first difficulty was getting the food from the plate or container into my mouth using my left hand to hold the fork or spoon. (If you're right-handed, try experimenting with the process yourself, keeping your right hand under the table and using only your left hand for everything.) Once the food got into my mouth, another set of obstacles was encountered. Half of my tongue and right cheek were numb, a sensation similar to receiving novocaine at the dentist. I had to be very careful not to bite down on my tongue or cheek instead of the food.

The final difficulty I faced during eating was learning that when one cannot feel, one cannot tell when food is stuck on one's face or that saliva may be coming from one's mouth. To this day I still shudder with remembrance and try to be extra careful to wipe my mouth repeatedly when eating in the company of other people.

A stroke victim is a person who is suddenly transformed from a competent, civilized adult into a slobbering, infantile creature stripped of standard everyday skills and normal dignity. I was frustrated and humiliated. Though I could not see myself at the table, I had seen my fellow patients in the rehabilitation hospital dining room and I knew that I was no different from them. There was an underlying sense of denial and outrage as I faced my difficulties day after day.

Time and time again I was forced into a state of humility. It was a humbleness I never before experienced. This disease had stripped me of all external dignity, grace, and competence. I had severe brain damage and physical disability. Now, I had no choice but to identify, for the first time in my life, with the physically handicapped, with the brain-damaged who cannot speak coherently and cannot perform elementary tasks. I was stripped of my vanity and ego, stripped of my pride and intellectual capacity. I, who had worked so hard for a master's degree in communication, could not speak a full sentence that anyone else in this world was able to understand. I was cocooned in a body that didn't work, with a mind that felt like a pinball machine gone whacko.

In this shadow time of my life, as I gradually began to really understand what had happened to me, a haunting realization surfaced. In the hospital the doctors questioned me as thoroughly as they could about possible causes of my stroke. They were interested in what might have been a source of original damage to the left carotid artery in my neck since I had no history of high blood pressure or high cholesterol. They asked me about a car accident or a neck injury. I had experienced none. The only incident I could think of was a violent argument my mother and I had when I was thirteen years old. She had been drinking at the time and flew into a rage.

I recalled this incident in the book *Mommie Dearest*, not knowing at the time I wrote about it that I would later have a stroke:

> She leaped off the counter and grabbed for my throat like a mad dog...like a wild beast...with a look in her eyes that will never be erased from my memory. I was caught totally defenseless and staggered backward, carried by her weight and momentum. I lost my footing and fell to the floor, hitting my head on the ice chest as I went down. The choking pain of her fingers around my throat met the thudding ache of the blow to the back of my head...
>
> "All I could think of was that my own mother was trying to kill me...She was terribly strong and all I could do was concentrate on loosening her grip on my throat.

But now I couldn't dwell on that past horror for very long because it was so terrifying. I had to concentrate only on the fact that I was alive and able to make progress. It couldn't matter that the process was physically slow and psychologically painful. The fact remained that I had been given the privilege of life itself. Anything less than gratitude was unacceptable. Although many times I felt like succumbing to negative, destructive feelings and impulses, I knew there was no room for self-pity, no place for depression. Too much work was yet to be done and my energy was not abundant enough to waste.

Two therapists visited me at home several days a week for several months. Each gave me "homework" to accomplish two or three times a *day* in their absence. I learned to take the attitude that my life was like being back at school or in summer camp.

The speech therapist worked with me on correctly pronouncing all the letters properly, paying special attention to the ones with which I was having difficulty, like *s* and *th* sounds.

We read sentences aloud together. From her I learned to pick up intonation and a sense of pacing, which it seemed I had lost. I tended to give each word the same emphasis, which created a flat-sounding speech pattern. My instincts had faltered. Speaking with a natural rhythm and tone had to be relearned. After the team reading, I read short sentences aloud by myself and told her what I thought they meant. With brain damage, I could recognize some individual words, but when they were strung together in a sentence they still held little meaning for me.

This last area was the one in which I could begin to see progress before the therapist could. In the hospital I had not been able to understand a sentence as simple as "The cat ran after the dog." I had some comprehension of a few individual words in the child's preschool book staring back at me through my tears, but when the words, printed in oversized letters, were marching along one after the other, I stared at them with no idea what they were trying to tell me.

Four or five weeks later, I was beginning to understand these very simple sentences. Once again they held some meaning. On a rudimentary level, my cognitive powers were being reprogrammed in my brain. I was instructed to read aloud every day for at least fifteen minutes. I was grateful for the years I had spent training to be an actress. This process had a ring of familiarity to it and with the familiar came a little comfort.

I also asked people to read aloud for me. The human voice has a very soothing quality that helps one to relax while going through a rigorous recovery process.

I enjoyed hearing someone read aloud. My nurse read biblical passages and my husband read from the newspaper. Today it is something I remember when visiting others in the hospital. Often I will inquire if they would like me to read to them. Most look surprised and seem pleased, indicating no one else had thought to ask the question or volunteer the service. It makes visiting time more pleasant and meaningful.

The occupational therapist taught me simple exercises to help strengthen and coordinate the use of my right hand. For instance, I learned to shuffle a deck of playing cards. Another exercise was to pick up clothespins with my thumb and forefinger and then line them up, clipped on a box edge. Some days she asked me to close my eyes and try to guess the different shapes or textures of objects she placed in my open palm. In the hospital I had not been able to distinguish the shape of a ball from that of a block, nor the feeling of cloth as opposed to metal without looking. It was still difficult.

We tackled the problem of dressing and taking care of myself. She showed me tricks for doing buttons with my right hand. To this day I still have trouble with buttons. It took six months more for me to put on my pierced earrings by myself in less than five or ten minutes and almost two years before I could use a typewriter again.

I could not use my two hands in concert with each other behind my back so I was taught how to fasten my bra in front and turn it around. I learned to choose clothes from my closet that posed a minimal challenge and didn't require the assistance of another person. After a while it is tiring to have to wait until someone can help you. In turn I perceived it was becoming annoying for David to have to assist me month after month after month.

Finally, the occupational therapist and I turned our attention to the household environment.

Our family was most fortunate to have Maria living with us. She was a college student who helped with housework, but I wanted to relearn the fundamentals of housekeeping anyway.

Because I was still unsteady walking by myself, I needed to approach doorways carefully, being aware that I should go through the middle of the opening in order not to risk bruising my right side without realizing it. Doors were *never* to be closed carelessly behind me. I could easily slam my hand in the closing door and seriously injure myself, once again due to a combination of diminished feeling and lack of accurate bodily perception. I had to pay attention to every detail.

* * *

The process of becoming ambidextrous began. My left hand could perceive sensitive movements such as turning the key properly to open a lock, winding a watch to the correct tightness, putting adequate pressure on touch-tone telephone buttons. These were only some of the operations that were not possible with the right hand, which I had normally used previously.

Tasks requiring two hands in complementary actions were very difficult, if not temporarily impossible. There is a saying that our fingers have an extra sensitivity—that we have "eyes in our fingers." At one extreme I imagine this as the talent displayed by safecrackers in the movies who use these eyes in their fingers to figure out combination-lock numbers on the big bank safes. At the other end of the spectrum, I think it is a talent most of us possess—"seeing" things with the sensitive touch of our fingers. Tasks such as locating hooks and eyes or buttonholes on the backs of our clothing and making the fasteners work are common practices that most of us take for granted. I couldn't do them.

The kitchen was fraught with potential dangers and the place where I needed the most help. I loved to cook and had done the majority of the cooking before my illness, even with the housekeeper present.

In addition to lacking sensation in my right arm, I was unable to distinguish between hot and cold. It was necessary for me to test the temperature of pots, pans, and water with my left hand first. The danger was that I could burn the skin on my right hand or arm and not know it, but the wound would still be serious.

The biggest surprise of relearning how to behave in my own kitchen came when I tried to follow the first new recipe.

It was at that moment that I came face-to-face once more

with the fundamental realization that I no longer had the same mental ability I had had before my stroke. Maybe I, too, persisted in thinking that the brain damage I had suffered was a much less serious condition, like the flu. Maybe I still imagined it as something I would live through uncomfortably for a short time, but if I was a good patient and did all the exercises wholeheartedly suddenly one day I would wake up totally well again. I guess it is a form of denial, sort of a well-intended self-preservation trick that simply does not work.

That particular day, standing in my kitchen, confused, anxious, and nervous, unable to follow simple recipe directions in systematic order, I realized finally that I was *not* the same. Maybe I would never be the same. Instead, I was on a very long, very difficult journey without benefit of a map to guide me through the unfamiliar territory.

There were a few close friends at my house that afternoon sitting outside in the garden. After I wiped away my tears and sat silently with my feelings, I then walked outside and asked someone to help me. Of course, they were more than happy to assist and pitched in quite naturally. I watched in awe. They made it seem so easy, so natural.

My previous life had taught me to be self-sufficient, *not* to rely on others, to value my independence. As an adult I had felt the need to be in control of my immediate environment, perhaps because during my childhood, life around me had been in chaos.

It made me very uncomfortable to ask for help, to admit I couldn't manage, to acknowledge my personal vulnerability. In fact, being helpless or vulnerable — my least favorite conditions — brought on a feeling of anxiety, a sense of failure.

I was very disappointed about my physical disabilities, but it was my mental incapacity that brought me anguish. The skills that had always served me well were my intellectual brightness, my agile mind and the ability to learn material easily. I had always been proud of that part of me and I had received many rewards from the outside world for exercising those talents. Now it was all gone. Today, I was a person who was not able to follow a simple recipe for a party dip!

A wave of great sadness swept over me. Humility stared me in the face, challenging me to accept the tough road given me. I stared back, bewildered and confused. Caught between pride and bereavement, I was stubbornly refusing to acknowledge the truth. The truth was *I had suffered severe brain damage.* I was going to have to learn to live with that fact and I didn't know how.

The next time the occupational therapist came to the house, I told her about what had happened with the recipe and asked her how to cope with the situation. As I related the incident I could feel a lump forming in my throat, tears welling up in my eyes and the flush of embarrassment on my face.

Calmly, she showed me how to segment one task into many tiny component parts in order to deal with them, one by one. She taught me to allot twice the time for any task so that I wouldn't create any unnecessary stress for myself. Hurrying she said, was an enemy of mine.

It's hard to put the physical feelings into words, but brain damage feels like being very nervous all the time, even if nothing is going on. When you *add* real stress of any sort, such as a physical struggle to accomplish a task or the mental strain of hurrying, the entire physical/mental system experiences "overload" symptoms. Then, any physical task or personal interaction becomes almost impossibly difficult. Irrational anger or sadness and frustration take over and everything suddenly becomes overwhelming. Under such circumstances nothing can be accomplished.

In order to cope with these feelings, I learned that I had to stop everything immediately. Then I had to sit quietly by myself. It was a real struggle to get back my equilibrium. I learned a phrase to be said quietly with the eyes closed, while doing slow, deep breathing. It calms me down and instills a feeling of peacefulness. Sometimes out loud and often to myself I have said: "Be still...and know I am God."

The former person, *me*, who was so quick to understand complicated problems and feel superior because of that skill, was at the present moment not an equal to a mentally retarded person. The old saying of not judging until you walk in the other person's shoes was coming home to me in full force.

Seemingly through no conscious choice of my own, I had been given the opportunity to experience being a physically and mentally handicapped person. In one life-moment flash of reality I understood the courage, patience and determination developed by handicapped people. I also recognized the special dignity with which they faced everyday life. It was an incredible transcendence. Though, admittedly, I tried to retain former images of myself, those images were burned away daily by the fire of a new reality.

Eventually I ceased expending energy struggling against acceptance of my condition. I concentrated instead on doing the best I could each day to make some progress in my recovery. I also stopped thinking in long-range terms. Each day, each moment, was important. I began expressing my gratitude just for being alive and not imposing a burden on my husband or others.

TWO CHRISTINAS

TWO MAJOR EVENTS took place in the fall of 1981. The Paramount film version of *Mommie Dearest* was released to theaters all over the country and my second book, a novel titled *Black Widow,* was being published in hardcover.

There were now two distinctly different Christinas. One —in the movie, perhaps distorted, but a public person, even an international celebrity. She is also referred to as the "children's advocate," the "breaker of taboo," the "ungrateful child," the "willful daughter," the "pioneer."

The other Christina bore absolutely no resemblance to the first perception. She is a bald, speechless spirit swimming slowly through the mist of life force sometimes here on earth, sometimes being carried through unknown parts of the universe. She can see with eyes, irises of green, seeing but the mist through different vision for which she can formulate no words, to which she cannot convey meaning yet.

The one Christina is so much a part of the struggle, tied, earthbound in emotions of fear, anger, mistrust. She is so radical, controversial a messenger of trust, having never learned to love.

The other creature is a soul returning from a long journey, back through eons of time, coming home once again, bringing the vision lost for millennia.

Perhaps there were always two Christinas. One of public perception, one of private dreams. One bound with chains of fear, another wishing on stars for deliverance.

Trust or die. Nurture or succumb. Learn to love or cease to be. There are now no other choices. We are on the second act of life's play. The first-act curtain has surely descended. An intermission has been experienced. And now the curtain lifts again slowly. The second act is up to you. You may weave the plot, tell the story, create the characters and choose the ending. It's up to you.

Afterwards we will all go home. Until then, you choose which Christina you will bring along.

Who will she be? How will she look? What will she feel?

Search all the illusions, seek all the dreams, cherish all the tears, kiss all the smiles, embrace the strength, the smallness, the vulnerability and open wide the door to her heart. For now, in this act, only love and the spirit will take her home. There is nothing else. No other existence is possible.

So search the illusions and you will see all the Christinas. Ask for the dreams and they, too, will come forth.

Only when the illusions and the dreams are one, in unity with the heart, will home appear. This is the second act. The process now is inescapably chosen. No straight and simple path is available. The map is here, it is part of what appears as illusions diminish. The illusions will persist until fear is relinquished. Fear leaves as love is learned.

And then, we're home again. Everyone wants to come

home. It is the great yearning underlying all our relationships, particularly with ourselves.

But for the moment, there were still these two Christinas.

David, who had worked on the *Mommie Dearest* film as executive producer, went to see a studio screening of the final edited version of the movie. He came home depressed and discouraged. The film tried to justify the bizarre behavior of Joan Crawford by blaming it on exterior events or the misdoings of her daughter. Many people had come to David privately and told him that the second screenplay I had written, with his help, was far superior to the script-by-committee and star that had been used for the film. Right now that was of little or no consolation.

David predicted that the film would not get good reviews. He was right. In fact, the film got bad reviews. Considering all the public relations–generated rumors before the film had been completed, which hinted that the star was giving an "Academy Award" performance, the reviews and public opinion were in ironic contrast.

David tried at first to keep the bad news about the film from me. I had been home from the hospital less than a month. He was under doctor's orders not to allow *any* stress or emotional upset to reach me. My condition, though temporarily stable, was nevertheless still precarious. There was absolutely no way for the medical team to predict whether or not the hospital treatment would continue to function adequately.

So, for the moment, David had to bear the brunt of all the disappointment, frustration and remorse over the way in which the film had been made.

David and I are convinced that people involved with the film didn't know the extent of their mistakes. What started out to be a serious drama became instead a "camp" classic.

Paramount then ran the "wire hanger" advertisement. Evidently the studio was trying to capitalize on the "camp" element the filmmakers had inadvertently attracted. But on October 6, 1981, Frank Yablans, the producer, filed suit against Paramount, requiring they remove his name from these ads.

The lawsuit charged: 1) "Breach of contract," 2) Intentional infliction of emotional distress, 3) "Breach of implied covenant of good faith and fair dealing," 4) (requested) temporary, preliminary and permanent injunction.

The ads were changed but the damage was done. For a long time the public remembered only the mistakes and the famous wire hangers. It hurt me personally, affected my reputation and damaged the cause of child-abuse prevention.

When I finally saw the picture with David in a small neighborhood theater that was nearly empty, my heart broke. What an incredible opportunity they had lost. This picture could have been a milestone. It could have been the very first film to delve into the problem of family violence from the point of view of the child. It could have explored the complex personal interactions of the mother and daughter, giving insight into the larger problem of child abuse. But it didn't. It was a series of hysterical scenes without explanation or relationship development.

Fortunately, on television, the smaller screen tended to camouflage and soften some of the more flagrant mistakes. My only consolation was that the book remained intact and complete. Hopefully, it was destined to be of longer duration than the film version. Only time would tell.

There were days during this period of my recovery when

it was very hard not to feel sorry for myself. There were other days when I failed that task entirely and sat with tears streaming down my face. Where was the hope and promise life had in store for me? It seemed to me that once more, everything had been taken away. Why? I wondered. Why?

Many times I felt like throwing the coloring book and the deck of cards through the window in a fit of frustration. Sometimes just the thought of having to get up on the exercycle bike for the thousandth time was enough to make me throw up. For a while I got so mad at not being able to use numbers correctly on the telephone, I refused to use the phone at all.

Worse still were the moments when I felt some weird sensation come over me. At those times panic set in, and I thought I was going to have another stroke. Inevitably it happened to me in a public situation such as the supermarket. Either I suddenly felt faint or my right hand would go numb. Those were the two danger signals I remembered from the first day when I went to the hospital.

These feelings are not the same as hypochondria (which is imagining an illness) nor are they the same as having an anxiety attack (which is feeling unexplained panic often accompanied by shortness of breath). I've experienced both hypochondria and anxiety attacks. Both are frightening intrusions into your life. Both are extremely difficult to explain to another person, particularly a person who has *not* had similar feelings. But the real uneasiness, the real lack of security with regard to the functioning of your own body is the terror of having your stroke in the first place.

The only other example I can think of is people caught in a sudden terrorist attack or perhaps a natural catastrophe that strikes without warning. But then, you are among *many* people who are in the same predicament. When you suffer a stroke there may be no warning, there may be no pain. When it hits, you are helpless. You are also all alone inside yourself.

PROGRESS

In November of 1981, my second book, a novel titled *Black Widow*, was published. David had arranged with the publishers for a short promotion tour. We were scheduled to begin in Los Angeles, which would enable me to become used to some public appearance pressure. The second stop was Chicago and the third was New York City.

My physical appearance was a stunning shock. My hair was half an inch long all over my head. The lack of hair made my eyes appear twice their usual size, giving my face a haunting quality. The public, including the majority of the media, were not aware that I'd had a stroke and consequently did not associate my peculiar hairstyle with my recent illness. Most people just thought I was being quite avant-garde, following a new European fashion. A few even asked what I thought of the punk-rock look and whether or not I'd consider adding green, purple or pink color to my hair!

In a way it was really quite hilarious. The magic of individual perception! Many times I laughed out loud, to the surprise of the interviewer. Some of them thought I was laughing at them and some probably just thought I was being weird. The laughter was really about myself. Previously I was concerned about my bald head and whether or not the large scar on the left side would show. Now I was being confronted with the image of myself as a punker! How wonderfully silly. What a good lesson in the foibles of vanity.

The winter of 1981–82 was one of the worst in recorded history. After New York, David and I attempted to continue the promotion tour to Washington, D.C. and then on to Atlanta. It had begun to snow in Washington that day and flights from National Airport were being canceled regularly. We finally made it out to Atlanta late in the afternoon. Several hours later we heard about the Air Florida plane that crashed in the Potomac River killing hundreds of people. It was only half an hour later than our flight.

We arrived in Atlanta during a freak blizzard. It took two hours to get from the airport to the Omni hotel. The entire city was at a standstill. No snow equipment, no transportation, no hot water or food. Our hotel was filled with convention people stuck without rooms. My husband met some cute girls in the lobby and thought about inviting them to share our room but used his better judgment at the last moment.

We were stuck in our room for almost two days until we could get a flight back to Los Angeles. That was the end of the book tour.

My husband had admittedly taken a risk talking me into attempting the tour so soon after my stroke. There was no guarantee I wouldn't fall apart. Some people thought he was pushing me too hard and that it would be detrimental for me.

But I am the sort of person who excels under adversity. That is the one condition of life with which I'm familiar since childhood. My entire being, my entire psyche is geared to deal with hard work and endless problem-solving. David knew me well enough to count on that facet of my personality.

When we came home, that new confidence gave me the courage to start dealing with a lot of other things I'd been afraid of all my life.

During our regular trips to the ranch in San Luis Obispo and partly because I was on my own most of the time, I began taking longer and longer walks into the far reaches of the countryside. For company I took the ranch dog, a black Labrador named Pepper. I also took Daisy, our ten-year-old grey and white terrier. The three of us explored the hills, the creeks and small hidden valleys on the property. Pepper knew the ranch well, having grown up there, and hunted successfully for her food. She and Daisy were great companions. Like all animal lovers, I felt no shyness about talking to the dogs as though they were people. The best thing of all for me was that the dogs paid absolutely no attention as to whether or not I said all the words correctly. It was great. I didn't feel alone because of their company and was able to chatter away without embarrassment or fear of making mistakes.

These wilderness walks became exhilarating experiences. They increased my stamina, my coordination and facility for negotiating uneven terrain. Sometimes I got carried away and became so engrossed with my surroundings that I paid no attention to where I was walking and promptly slipped or fell. There was protection in the padding from my heavy winter clothes and I was never hurt.

With Pepper and Daisy, I increased the walk to about five

miles each day, staying out in the back country for three and four hours at a time.

There was a sense of magic out there—freedom and order and incredible beauty. I was a visitor to this wilderness kingdom. Often I would sit quietly on a rock or a log, opening my perceptions for the gifts of sight, sound and awareness.

The dogs played games and chased rabbits. I watched proudly as though caring for my children at the park. The animals moved with such grace and efficiency that my recent tasks of regaining physical coordination enabled me to marvel in true appreciation at their effortless prowess.

Winter was still present. A bone chill stayed in the breeze all day. Mallard ducks had left the lake. The air was pungent crisp and the grass stayed damp till mid-morning.

Out here, I was free. Out here I was part of all the creatures who'd walked before me on these paths. Out here I first learned to accept who I had become.

The experience made me feel good about myself. Not just because the muscle tone was returning to my body; not just because I was conquering my fear of being alone in the wilderness; but because I was really alive, appreciating every moment of the fantastic gift I'd been given.

During the remainder of the first year after the stroke I regained the majority of my physical skills. Some feeling returned to the right side of my body. The reason I know full feeling had not returned was one of those strange bits of humor you get by accident. In the summertime, the bugs at the ranch are serious beasts. It was not long before I saw that only my right side was continuously marked by telltale red mosquito bites. The left side of my body was rarely bitten. The reason? I could feel the miserable insect on the left side and brush it off *before* it had a chance to bite me. I looked a little strange with bites only on one arm and leg but I was probably the only one who noticed!

The doctors had told me during my regular checkup that I could expect to see progress throughout the entire first year. I believe they meant that in a positive way. We live in a world of immediate gratification. People want to see results. I think the doctors were trying to let me know that my progress might be slow but that it would continue steadily through that first year.

It's true that during the first year I regained the majority of my physical skills—walking, talking, writing, caring for myself and accomplishing the normal tasks of everyday life. But I still had limited capacity for intellectual complexities. I still had little tolerance for stress and became easily frustrated or angry. But my progress was dramatic. In August, I had been unable to walk, talk or read. I had come so far. My hair had also grown enough so that I now had a regular short haircut and not my punk/avant garde look.

I had to get reading glasses for the first time because my eyesight had diminished. Comprehension of what I read was problematic. Retention, once I understood, was a bit better.

Finally the doctors permitted me to drive my car in the neighborhood on surface streets but not yet on the freeways. That was a great freedom ticket.

As the first year drew to a close, I tried to evaluate my progress. It was hard not to compare what I had been like before the stroke to my ability now. If, as the medical team indicated, this was to be the sum total of my progress, I was most fortunate. I could care for myself, drive a car, read and do simple work in the office and in the garden. I had to learn to accept this much with genuine gratitude and then keep trying for more. I had to live always right in the moment and focus on doing small tasks well.

But, to my surprise, the second year I began to regain the cognitive capacities with which I had been previously blessed. My memory for retention of new material began to return. My skill with numbers improved dramatically. I was now able to work with simple numerical problems in our own business and to make all of my own personal telephone calls, although I misdialed numbers continuously. My physical agility and stamina improved.

However, contrary to my previous nature, I had become totally dependent on my husband to negotiate the outside world for me. I tired quickly from being with people. It wasn't a case of not liking others, rather it was the strain of relating and retaining information. It was just easier to be alone.

In contrast, David was a very gregarious man and being tied to me, to my frailties and lack of staying-power, was getting to be very annoying. He needed fun and more lively companionship.

My perception of myself at this point was definitely not that of a "fun person." For the first time since my teenage high-school years, I found myself battling twinges of jealousy when I saw David obviously enjoying himself with others. It was a kind of fun I couldn't seem to join, which left me feeling orphaned. I was unable to voice my complaint. I felt guilty because previously he'd been so comforting and loyal during the worst of my illness. How could I not wish him pleasure now? Those feelings put me in a position of resentment and further isolation. They made for unpleasantness, separateness and sharp tempers between us.

Our married life as adult sexual partners had also been

interrupted by my illness. After seeing me as an invalid, bald and incoherent, it was understandably difficult for my husband to relate to me as a sexual partner again, even after my recovery had progressed well into the second year.

I think that some tragedy is so shocking to one's psyche that a long time is required to erase its traumatic memory.

It was less difficult for me to make the ongoing adjustments because I didn't have to look at myself. My husband did. It was painful for him. He also resented being cast against his will into the role of nurse.

No one is initially comfortable thinking about sexual activity with an invalid. There's something repugnant and/or exploitive about the concept. But for the stroke victim who was not born with the incapacity and who feels like trying to regain normality, the situation is confusing, embarrassing, and difficult to discuss.

WILDERNESS WALK

ALL MY LIFE I was probably under too much stress. Even with success, life was beset with adversity. Each day could turn into a battle against the odds without much provocation. I was good at being an adversary. I knew how to fight.

Before my stroke I was aware of feeling exhausted by the unending confrontations. After my stroke, those confrontations, those battles were no longer acceptable conditions under which I wanted to live.

The numbness in my right hand became an early warning signal of impending stress, anger or fear. At the onset of the sensation, I immediately took steps to 1) calm down 2) remove myself from the confrontation 3) recognize the negative person or situation for future avoidance.

The phrase, "Be still...and know I am God" sounded over and over in my mind. It had the effect of bringing me peacefulness, calm, and serenity almost immediately.

This new way of life requires consciously changing the habits of twenty or thirty years. In the beginning you have to be prepared to walk out of rooms sometimes, or stop conversations in mid-sentence, and consciously avoid anger.

It is helpful to be aware that this form of self-protective action is contrary to established acceptable norms of communication between people. It may cause temporary confusion or even hostility in others. People may even think you're a little crazy. But until I learned to trust these alternate ways of interacting with people while also protecting my health, drastic measures did not seem unwarranted.

Every situation in life is given to us for the purpose of learning and growing. Certainly that was true of the personal early-warning system I had in my hand. The physical sensations were easy to recognize and I eventually learned to relate them to my emotions or feelings. Not only is it a better way for me to live as a stroke patient but it is a more productive way for me to live as a human being. Honestly, I wish there had been something similar before in my life so that I didn't have to wait for a stroke to learn these lessons about stress.

During the entire course of my recovery I learned to depend on my power of imagination. Many times during each day I would imagine myself whole and well. Although my hands were stiff and awkward, I saw them agile and strong. Although my footsteps were unsteady and my gait shuffling, I saw myself swimming in the pool and hiking easily through open fields.

While perspiration dripped down my face as I labored with a simple earring or a stubborn button for five or ten minutes at a time, I thanked God for letting me get this far in my progress.

I never, never gave up, no matter how many times I wanted to have a super temper tantrum!

Dr. Heifetz told me *not* to put sloppy habits into my brain. He told me to try my very best to do each task right, to say each word right, to walk with energy, to project positive thoughts.

Before you have much strength, you have imagination. You can "see" yourself doing the exercise correctly and then try to do it that way down to the smallest detail. First comes the concept, then the reality will follow.

The point here is not pure success or failure—it is rather a series of tiny, incremental steps *toward* achieving your goal, which for today may be no more than successfully touching thumb to forefinger. Those goals are your building blocks to freedom of movement and speech and thinking. If you build them carefully, consistently, they will hold the weight of your progress. Otherwise they will come crashing to the ground with the first real pressure, with the first stress that is applied.

Because of the brain's damage as a result of the stroke, even in recovery I was still volatile, easily upset, quick to anger and I cried at the drop of a hat. Therefore, in order to make progress, I had to learn that it is necessary to find a measure of serenity in my life, to spend part of my day cultivating serenity by *myself*, and *not* to expect someone else to bring serenity to me, like a tray of food or a bedpan.

It is also true that I have had to change my way of life in other areas. At first these changes were primarily because I had to lower my expectations about what was possible for me and to find happiness in the fact that I was alive and able to care for myself.

The doctors told me I had to quit smoking immediately. I quit smoking the day of my stroke and was warned by the doctors after the operation that I must never smoke again. They were afraid that I might have something wrong with my entire vascular system. If that were true, smoking would seriously aggravate my condition. I stopped eating red meat, took extra vitamins and became conscious of positive health habits on an everyday basis.

Because of the dyes and drugs that were injected into my body during the diagnostic and surgical periods of my illness, my entire physical system had changed. I had become allergic. I had unexpectedly severe reactions to both flu and tetanus shots after my stroke though I had never experienced those reactions before. I had also become allergic to alcohol, even to wine. I had never considered myself a big drinker. Nevertheless the lack of tolerance I had now for alcohol was acute, even though I was not yet fully prepared to recognize this fact.

Not drinking if you know you have an adverse reaction to alcohol sounds rational and reasonable. But it was still not an easy task for me. I felt as though I were once more facing failure and I was scared.

When I grew up, the "in" thing to do was smoke and drink. I had wanted to be a part of the group. So, I smoked and drank. Giving both up after my illness was another way of giving up parts of my old self-image. I wasn't yet comfortable with that person who didn't smoke. I certainly didn't know anything about a person who didn't drink. I had lived in a drug culture all my life. How was I going to have any fun? How was I going to go to parties or talk to people I'd just met? What was life to be like without my double crutches of cigarettes and alcohol? I succeeded in never smoking again. That same success was not true when it came to drinking.

In order for me to get well again, to rehabilitate myself from my stroke, I had to be my own primary focus, the single and solitary most important person in my life. This change in life focus was a great pendulum swing for me because always before I had been the caretaker of everyone else. The stroke and my recovery from it unalterably changed that pattern.

However, as I now made consistent progress, I realized that a terrible toll had been taken on my marriage and relationship with David. In an attempt to repair that damage, I agreed to accept a speaking engagement on a cruise ship, so that he and I could spend some relaxing, uninterrupted time together.

July 1984 was spent aboard the large ship *Norway*, cruising from Philadelphia to Europe. This was the third time I'd been asked to be a celebrity speaker for a cruise line and David and I thoroughly enjoyed the vacation. However, on this trip I could not deny or bridge a growing distance between my husband and me. I saw him drifting beyond my reach, beyond my ability to communicate.

When we returned via Amsterdam, the Los Angeles rat race commenced immediately. Despite jet lag, the next day I had to appear at a charity cocktail party and make a brief speech.

That wasn't unusual. I couldn't remember the last time I'd gone anywhere just as a guest. There was always some responsibility, a speech, fund-raising. Being a private person, invited somewhere, anywhere, was unknown to me. Everything seemed maneuvered, manipulated, calculated, the wheeling and dealing of power, fear, guilt, intimidation.

We arrived at Jimmy's restaurant in Beverly Hills on time. Between David and me there was an ominous silence that started by accident and rapidly became a metaphor for the entire relationship as our minds spun past "awful" into "catastrophic."

The speech, the cocktail party, were fine. The real-life disaster was dinner.

Ten of us sat down at a table in Jimmy's about nine P.M.. I

recall being pleased that I was feeling no ill effects from the several glasses of wine I'd had earlier. I remember ordering my meal, and virtually nothing else! I do not remember even having more wine to drink. I do not remember swearing at David, calling him a prick! I do not remember leaving the restaurant, nor coming home.

I do remember being violently, disgustingly sick in my bathroom. I do remember David helping me.

I do remember waking up at three A.M., sitting bolt upright in bed, nearly screaming in panic.

Something terrible had taken hold of my life. Please God, I prayed, don't let me become like my mother!

I shook and shook and rocked myself, clutching my knees.

Terror had struck. I got up, trying to steady myself, scared to death.

Please God, help me. I cried. Please, help me…I don't have any more courage…I don't have any more strength …I can't make it across another chasm…I'm exhausted trying to get well, to be good, take care of everything. Please…help me! I sat curled up in a living room chair, sobbing until my chest ached, feeling my heart shatter into even smaller pieces.

It was neverending. Putting myself back together was a relentless process.

Shaking so badly I could hardly manage the telephone, at nine o'clock that morning I called information for Alcoholics Anonymous.

"I need help," I heard myself saying. "Could you tell me where I can go to a meeting tonight?"

The woman on the phone offered to send someone to my house to help me but I was too mortified, too embarrassed to accept.

So, feeling like a real lunatic, I went to my first AA meeting all alone.

After pulling into the parking lot and sitting in my car until it was almost too late to be on time, I finally got up the nerve to go inside the church building where the meeting was being held.

I was never so terrified as I was walking through that door alone. I was sure everyone would know, that I couldn't pretend I was all right.

A woman introduced herself to me, took my hand and I burst into tears. I cried for the entire meeting.

This woman showed me how to choose another meeting for the following day and I left, never saying more than a few sentences.

Not having the faintest idea how to proceed, I just went to meetings each day and didn't drink.

At first I hated to think of myself as being at the meetings. Then very, very slowly I started feeling more comfortable. I started laughing again, instead of shutting myself off because I was ashamed by my own weaknesses.

David was relieved. He congratulated me, saying it was so much more pleasant to be around me without the anger and fighting.

But, I was still upset with him. I wanted him to change too. I wanted him to get a job and I wanted him to help support his family. My not drinking just meant we didn't argue over it every day.

In December David began a long series of business trips. He was gone three and four weeks at a time.

In his absence I had to take care of the paperwork, the bills, our company. We had a young secretary to help a few days a week but it was basically my responsibility.

Then there was the ranch. Every two weeks I drove up

north alone with my two new dogs, Pepper's puppies.

Now our walks in the wilderness were a sight to behold. One woman, four dogs.

Harkening back to images of Greek mythology, to the huntress Diana and her loyal dogs, hours and hours, mile upon mile we walked back further and further into the mountains, into the wilderness. In the cooler weather I left the beaten paths, left the safety of the well-worn cattle trails, narrow as they were, and ventured into the brush, across hills and into small canyons hidden from view.

When it is cold, the rattlesnakes hibernate and are not a threat. As the day warmed, I rattled keys as a warning of my approach and the dogs always went ahead, fanning out, flushing the bush in true bird-dog fashion.

I loved to watch them. I loved these walks. My feet were now connected to this earth. The rocks had faces like people in a crowded hall. The trees whispered to me as I sat marveling at their intricate symphony. Hawks, golden in the afternoon sun, soared effortlessly on an unseen gust of air. The blue heron, long legs always dangling a bit behind, searched and swooped seeking, always seeking. Red-winged blackbirds abounded, flashing across the sky. Carniverous magpies pecked at a dead ground squirrel.

The dogs barked in that special voice telling me they were tracking a jackrabbit, chasing through the thick chaparral underbrush.

I watched the dogs, the trees, the birds, the clouds, the movement of wind, the sun, the shadows, the insects, the flowers. I accepted their gifts of smell, of coolness, of groundedness, of warm comfort, of sound, of wisdom.

So freely they gave. So generous, so boundless, so unselfish.

Yet it occurred to me that this wilderness, this wild land

always seeks to take back its own. Nature takes her own back into herself. The mother earth bosom embraces all who are of her.

City people can't understand that phenomenon. They see land only for what it can do to benefit their pocketbook. So, they don't see anything they didn't already bring with them.

After two years, the land finally began to be open to me. My eyes, my ears, my mind no longer brought only preconceived notions. I was no longer a stranger here.

Many, many times I got down on my knees, dogs scattered around, priestesses incarnate, praying for help, for understanding, for deliverance from attachment to the past, for release from all anger and hatred for those who did me harm. I held onto the earth with my fingers as one would clasp the hand of a friend.

There was a person in my world for whom I felt real hatred. I prayed for release from them, from my own hatred, tears often streaming down my face.

"Please God, release me—allow me to understand."

I knew then that this land and I wouldn't be together as I had imagined before. I would have to say good-bye to this land I loved. I would never build a house here. I would not live out long years underneath the trees in the grove of whispering digger pines.

These were the years of my personal vision quest in the wilderness. These years were the beginning of my transformation. Alone, I went into the wilderness asking the land and the universe for the gift of understanding, of release from old patterns, for the miracle of connectedness of my spirit with the universe itself. And the mother earth, the universe began to show me how to find the answers.

WAKING UP

I WAS NOT yet able to see in relationships that we tend to hypnotize each other all the time. The words we say to one another, the phrases we repeat over and over, the negative suggestions, are all part of the series of hypnotic messages that become a lifestyle.

We program one another to be a certain way, to agree upon preferred behavior, to deny the existence of some flaws, to administer justice and to meet needs.

It is all hypnosis. It is a dream, an illusion of relationship.

We become the given total of combined faults, one building on the other like the giant African termite mounds on the open plains.

We camouflage, we cover, we hide behind the other, we play the adult episode of "attack-and-retreat," which has replaced our childhood game of "hide-and-seek."

Then comes the belief that outside events shape our lives.

When a deal goes sour or a job ceases or a business fails, we see the event as compounding the hypnosis, pulling and tugging at us as though our lives were corks bobbing around in a restless sea.

The better we are at maintaining the struggle, the longer it takes for the hypnotic relationship to unravel. It takes so long because we agree to stay "stuck" in the constant tension of struggle that keeps the relationship going. The guiding principle is: keep chaos current!

Perhaps one day, the critical thread breaks. Something no bigger than a moth hole will do it. Like a match flame eating through old paper, the relationship disintegrates, changing shape and form, color and texture in the process.

The hypnosis is over. You are wide awake. Wide awake. Wide awake in a world you never expected, nor anticipated being in.

Waking up is a shock. Waking up feels different. Part of the shock is the realization of "before," the realization of the hypnosis, of the sleep, of the dream state you agreed to live in for all that past time.

Where was I? How could I have allowed this to happen? Why did it go on so long? Where was my head?

Another part of the shock is embarrassment. Everyone will know it didn't work out. A sense of failure, the loss and hurt all rolled up into wordless shame.

At the end of May 1985, just before Memorial Day weekend, I helped my husband pack his clothes into the silver Honda sedan, kissed him good-bye, wished him a safe journey, and watched as he drove down the driveway, into the street, and off to Chicago.

Instead of reacting with anger, an almost incurable sadness rolled over me as I watched him disappear. Once again I was reminded that everyone I ever loved either had been taken away or had left me.

The house was empty. My stepson was in the last year of college. It is just a matter of time before my marriage to David is finally over, I thought. Even though he returned from Chicago on a regular basis, emotionally David never came home again. He was gone. The dream was over. The illusion had disappeared.

What will I do with my life?

How will I manage?

Why continue?

It seems I've been here before. This place of hopelessness and despair. It seems as though it's always waiting for me when I am through with the excitement and the people.

Why is that? Why do I keep returning to this place? Why do I have these feelings of isolation, abandonment?

A few days later I stopped by the office of my homeopathic physician to pick up some nutritional supplements I couldn't get elsewhere. I had no appointment with the doctor but when he saw me at the counter, he asked me to come back in an hour to talk.

We sat outside on the rooftop garden as the afternoon sun faded behind the nearby taller buildings.

"I feel like I'm preserving a body without knowing why ...like I have a responsibility for staying alive even though I don't know for what purpose."

He nodded his head, indicating he understood what I was trying to explain. He was the same doctor who had suggested I read Ruth Montgomery's book *Strangers Among Us* about "walk-ins" after he learned about my stroke, the operation, brain damage and my recovery. He never knew me before the illness and had not seen me until three years into my recovery, which by then was almost complete.

Two things had amazed him. One was my general overall state of health, which he said was amazingly excellent. The other was my physical appearance and the fact that he couldn't believe I was forty-six years old. That was a nice compliment since he said I looked ten years younger.

"I know you believe in reincarnation," he said quietly. "Do you also believe in God?"

"Yes," I answered, puzzled.

"What about faith?" he continued. "Could this process you describe be a test of faith?"

"A test of faith?" That seemed such a simple idea, until I really thought about it. Faith is what one has in the face of nothing else. When there's no rational explanation, one continues to persist through faith.

One can even confront the void itself accompanied only by faith.

Faith was not such a simple idea after all.

Two months later, during July 1985, I finally woke up totally. It takes a while for the years of hypnosis to wear off. The feeling was as clear as waking up one morning from a dream, maybe from a nightmare, maybe even from another lifetime.

Suddenly, the light dawned and reality came flooding into my consciousness with information and a barrage of unpleasant realizations.

My husband had left me . . . with no money, lots of debts, a string of failures and a sense of personal humiliation that suffocated me.

He had left me in order to save himself. I understood that part. What I couldn't understand is how I had let myself get into this horrible predicament.

For the years since my illness, I had been emotionally hypnotized and I had watched as the disasters mounted up, coming closer and closer to the moment of destruction.

During that time, I couldn't seem to save myself. I

couldn't seem to effect any protection of myself. I felt immobilized, helplessly watching my own demise, yet somehow being forced to participate in it against my will.

That was the worst part. The feeling that I had participated in my own demise. Like watching your own death in slow motion, seeing the killer but unable to scream or flee from danger.

That sense of participation caused me to blame myself. After all, I was an adult. I could have said *no*.

I did say *no*. I said *no* over and over and over again—but it was not effective.

I screamed and bitched. We argued and then he did what he wanted and the disaster continued.

When I fully awoke that day in July, it was with a sense of horror.

What would become of me? What would I do? I felt so alone.

My stroke, my past, my success, my disorientation toward people, had all worked in concert to isolate me from the rest of the world.

I was forty-six years old and didn't know how to be a person! I didn't know who I was!

Of course I knew how to *do* lots of things. My entire life was built on competence. Competence was my defense system, my shield against feeling and hurting and sharing and failing and vulnerability. Competence was always good enough in the past. I took easily to courage and leadership, but those were easy for me too, far easier than sharing, than asking, than intimacy or than "not knowing". Rather than admit not knowing, I would simply not participate. Then no one would realize my ignorance or my feelings of inadequacy.

Why? Vulnerability in my lexicon means ammunition, ammunition which is given to the enemy with which to annihilate. So, vulnerability equals annihilation.

Simple equation. Even more simple to avoid at all costs. Simple, therefore, to live your life without intimate friends, close relationships, without much love.

In fact, the highest cost of this deceptively simple equation is the loss of love. It is, indeed, a high price to be paid in return for daily survival.

But, when, as an adult, you can't get your needs met because as a child no one was there to validate and love you and you never developed interpersonal life skills, that is how you live. At least that is how I lived.

So, when it was over and I woke up from my dream of "how it might be" and saw that it wasn't, everything came tumbling to the ground all at once.

EARTH MOTHER

RUTH MONTGOMERY'S BOOK *Strangers Among Us* intrigued me enormously when I finally bought it from the Bodhi Tree bookstore in West Hollywood and read it in just two sittings.

The concept of "walk-in" fascinated me. The author explains that a walk-in is a soul/person who has an important mission to accomplish on earth, usually to improve human communication and unity. This soul/person doesn't feel the need to wait until it can go through birth, infancy, adolescence. So it works out an arrangement with another soul/person who wants to leave this earth but not by the suicide route.

As I understood the idea from her book, the two souls make a bargain to change places using one body as a vehicle. This is *not* the same idea as "possession." Rather, it is like changing drivers using the same car.

The exchange happens during times of accident, trauma or serious illness. It might explain some of the pronounced "personality" changes after such a "near death" experience.

I was intrigued specifically because of what the homeopathic doctor said to me earlier and because I myself felt like such an entirely different person after my stroke. I even photographed differently. I was much more beautiful. My eyes were a truly astonishing green color, sparkling like deep forest pools filled with magic and mystery. I enjoyed my body, took more loving care of it and enjoyed being female, which I'd not done before.

The author listed ways of reaching some of the people she'd interviewed or researched who had been identified as walk-ins.

One was a man who had a metaphysical organization in Malibu, California. I wrote to him.

A few weeks later, information on Dick Sutphen, his books, tapes and lectures arrived in the mail. He was a good choice for me because he was a prolific writer and very active lecturer.

He wasn't giving any more seminars in the California region for the rest of the year. I was disappointed until I noticed that there was a weekend seminar in Dallas listed for the end of October.

That same day I called to register and made my airline reservations.

Shortly afterward, my friend Kiki Borlenghi and I were off to Italy for the Mifed film market in Milan. I had one of those frequent-flyer free tickets good from the U.S. to Paris and she had relatives in Milan.

It was a great trip. Ten whirlwind days in Europe and back home. We'd each worn out one pair of shoes walking the length and breadth of magical Florence, where we went for three days after Milan.

Before leaving, I had picked up my tickets for the Sutphen seminar in Dallas.

When I came home and looked for them, the tickets had vanished.

It was necessary to sit down with myself and think carefully about the meaning of this strange turn of events.

Was this an indication that I shouldn't go to the seminar?

Or, were the missing tickets a test to see how serious my decision was to pursue the path of new answers?

It was a dilemma. Not only wasn't I sure about the meaning of the event, I didn't really think I could afford full-fare airline tickets. The lost ones had been a bargain fare, about half as much.

The next day I went to the airline, filled out the lost-ticket voucher information and flew standby coach to Dallas.

Another good decision.

The two-day seminar was called "Create Your Own Reality."

Richard Sutphen is an accomplished group leader and metaphysician.

The room held about 250 to 300 people. Most were nicely dressed, middle-class without any alarming trappings of what Sutphen calls "metaphysical frou-frou!"

His sense of humor was also refreshing. He seemed extremely ethical, both in the words he expressed and in the behavior of his organization.

The seminar only cost seventy-nine dollars for two days! His intent was to give the information he has to as many people as possible, which became obvious as the hours rolled by. He also didn't want to be a metaphysical guru, and said so openly.

The whole point was for each of us to take our own responsibility for life and for finding the answers within ourselves, not outside in another person or anything else.

I have long thought that we're such an "other-directed

CHRISTINA CRAWFORD

culture," such a "take-a-pill-and-fix-your-feelings" society, that it was easy for me to agree with him.

The interesting work was learning to use the tools he gave us for traveling the road within.

He taught us hypnosis and past life regression as well as the principles of reincarnation and karma.

Two days later I flew back to L.A. with a whole new insight into the incredible richness of this journey I had embarked upon. What is extraordinary to experience is the sensation of doors finally opening into vast storehouses filled with knowledge, wisdom and teachers. Hard for one to comprehend is that this treasure awaits all of us who seek it with an open heart.

On February 13, 1986, just one day before my tenth wedding anniversary, I signed the papers, filing for dissolution of my marriage to David.

It was a day of sadness, a day I never thought would come to me again. This would be my second divorce. A day not originally of my conscious choosing, but now a day of my intention. At least it was a day of reality, a day that marked the beginning of a process that had a prescribed ending and therefore it was a day of release.

Being totally responsible for your life is not an easy course to learn. You want to take credit for the good things and still be able to blame someone else for the fuck-ups.

It is awesome to realize we choose it all—the family we're born into, the health we have, the career we pursue, the hurdles we battle, the mistakes we make, and the victories we enjoy.

This journey to find the path of my soul is not linear, but has arrived in strange bits and pieces, traveled in fits and starts, taken tangential side trips and even a few false avenues. It has been both active and dormant. It has waited patiently for me to find out that I have no other choice but to embark fully and pursue it wholeheartedly.

My initial introduction to reincarnation occurred when, as a seventeen-year-old college freshman, someone gave me a copy of *The Prophet* by Kahlil Gibran. Instantly some part of me recognized that this philosophy was the only reasonable explanation for the suffering and chaotic condition of my young life. My mother and I were chosen by one another to play out some karmic drama as yet not understood by me.

While as a young teenager my knowledge remained rudimentary, my sense of relief that there existed some universal explanation was fundamental to my ability to proceed while living under what I felt were intolerable conditions.

The *Baghavad-Gita* made the rounds of the hippie community several years later in Laurel Canyon, where I, in my early twenties, was also introduced to the writings of Krishnamurti.

Because I originally thought Krishnamurti a writer of the past, it was a surprise to be invited to hear him speak in person at Santa Monica Civic Auditorium by the woman who had taught me a transcendental meditation at that time. The reason I started meditating was that it was supposed to help you learn more rapidly. I was then thirty-three years old, taking twenty units each quarter at UCLA and in the process of completing three years of undergraduate work in one and a half years.

A few years later still, I would take carloads of friends and fellow students from graduate school along with my husband David to Ojai where we were privileged to sit outside under the majestic oak trees and listen to this physically diminutive Indian man, Krishnamurti, who was such a brilliant mind and soaring spirit.

In fact the annual trek to Ojai went on for several years,

until Krishnamurti was no longer able to speak. He died soon thereafter.

In Dick Sutphen I recognized that same combination of personal calm and sense of urgency about the teachings as I'd seen years before in Krishnamurti.

It took Dick Sutphen's earthy approach to put it all together in a way that made complex ideas seem clear but not trivialized. He used a unique combination of communication technology and old-fashioned charisma to get information across.

While in Dallas, we received information on the Easter trip to the vortexes in Sedona, Arizona.

Legend has it that there are four primary energy vortexes on the earth. They are spiritual power spots or sites of increased metaphysical energy. Two of these sites are said to be positive centers. These are located in Sedona, Arizona and Kaui, Hawaii. The two negative centers are located in the Bermuda Triangle and Sussex County, England. These power centers are connected through lines of energy, called ley lines, to other power spots on earth such as Stonehenge.

These ley lines have been documented throughout the world, through the field of learning called geomancy which means "sacred layout of the landscape." They are perhaps similar in concept to the meridians in the human body along which lie the acupuncture points described in Chinese medicine and through which flows the energy called chi.

The idea is that these power spots, these vortex places and the Sedona vortexes in particular, have increased energy. When people enter one of the vortex areas this increased energy affects their individual vibrational rate.

A basic metaphysical principle indicates that personal vibrational rate increases with spiritual development and evolution.

Entering the increased energy of the vortex may bring experiences of heightened awareness and higher consciousness awakening. It might even provide spiritual information to those sitting in quiet meditation within the vortex or even at its perimeter.

The whole idea seemed too exciting to miss. So, experiencing the Sedona vortexes became part of my future plans.

Where the money would come to do all this was still a mystery.

However, it was becoming increasingly clear to me that right now there was nothing more important than my own transformation. In fact, I was the only one responsible for the transformation.

Once on the track, nothing would dislodge me. I'd been standing in the middle of a place called Lost too long not to know that slowly, very slowly, the doors of perception were beginning to open for me.

Despair was still my companion, but no longer a daily visitor.

Now my concern revolved around how it was going to be possible to clear up the rest of the debts, sell my portion of the ranch, find my way into new productivity that would sustain me. The answers were still illusive.

In the meantime, there were speaking engagements for which I was well paid and enjoyed doing. People contacted me to speak on the subjects of child-abuse prevention, family violence or adult survivors of childhood abuse and the issue of personal empowerment at large fund-raising events or state conferences. It gave me a wonderful opportunity to see parts of the country that I might not otherwise visit and most importantly, hear different points of view, learn from other experiences and meet wonderful, dedicated people.

It also kept me focused and current. As a commissioner for Children's Services in Los Angeles County since 1984, I received a tremendous amount of information constantly but traveling to other parts of the country, other states, gave me a much better perspective of the entire national picture.

Easter weekend, 1986, a psychologist friend and I flew to Phoenix and drove a rental car to Sedona, Arizona.

She and I were booked into a motel called Cedar Resort and shared a nonsmoking room. When we were unpacking that night I thought I heard the sound of water but couldn't see anything from our balcony when I stood there piercing my eyes into the black night.

The next morning, curious to see where we were, I ventured out into the balcony once more to be greeted by a spectacular sight.

Our motel was situated directly over Oak Creek, a beautiful river running through the heart of Old Sedona.

My heart leaped at the unexpected beauty of the river and of this morning.

What a metaphor for this part of my journey.

How like my life, so filled with night, so few clues.

Filled with despair almost half of the time, questioning myself, my life, the purpose for continuing at all, was like our nighttime arrival and staring out into the impenetrable darkness, with only the sound of water to intrigue me.

Yet, this morning, here we are, here I am, stunned speechless by the power and tranquility of this place.

We went across the street to a coffee shop for breakfast where you could smell the fresh biscuits and country pan gravy.

Though years ago my mother made one film in Sedona, a western titled *Johnny Guitar* for Republic Studios, I never was here before.

The land is astonishing. The soil and the mountains are the color of red clay. The trees are technicolor green and streams run crystal-clear blue.

Old Sedona is a western town with Indian jewelry stores and art galleries and souvenir shops.

The local population is as interesting as the movies that used to be made there. Originally there were native Indians, then came ranchers and cowboys, later the movie people and artists and finally psychics, metaphysical sorts and nouvelle cuisine restaurants.

After a seminar session the first day we went to Airport Mesa vortex with a map given to us by the Sutphen organization and admonitions to watch out for rattlesnakes and scorpions.

Even after a thorough explanation of the power of the vortex places, I still felt a sense of awe.

Where had I been all these years, not to know anything about this, I wondered.

Since my fear of heights made me uncomfortable inching along the rim path of Airport Vortex, I did not follow my friend out to the middle of the vortex circle but stayed on the wider entrance to do my meditation.

There were other people from the group, all were respectfully quiet as they chose places to sit down.

The sun was setting and it was pleasantly cool.

After an undetermined amount of time sitting cross-legged with my eyes closed in meditation, I felt someone standing near me.

When my eyes opened I saw my friend, looking ashen and visibly shaken.

"What is it?" I whispered so as not to disturb others.

"Let's go," she replied.

"Are you all right?"

"I'll tell you in the car," she said, already heading down the steep hill toward the rental car, which was parked parallel to the road.

Once inside the car, I asked her again if she was all right.

Although a healthy skeptic, this woman is a brilliant psychotherapist and my friend of fourteen years. She's not an alarmist, nor prone to hallucination.

Airport Vortex is said to be electric energy, masculine persuasion. Bell Rock is magnetic energy, female orientation. The Mother Earth Vortex, largest of the vortex power spots, is said to be a balance of electromagnetic and male-female energy.

My friend told me that while she was sitting in meditation, an energy attached to her that felt as though it were threatening to push her off or pull her over the cliff edge and into the vortex canyon hundreds of feet below.

Whether she actually verbalized it or whether I thought it, the information indicated it was "grandfather" energy and very powerful.

Sutphen had alerted us to the unusual quality of power, energy in these vortex places. My friend knew to extricate herself quickly, yet she said she could hardly move and had to use all her strength of will to crawl back to the wide flat entrance where I waited, totally unaware of the drama taking place just a few hundred feet away.

On Easter Sunday morning I arose before sunrise, dressed quietly and left for the drive to the huge Mother Earth Vortex about ten miles away.

When we'd gone earlier, the echo-effect from people talking and walking was distracting and I felt as though I wanted to return alone, spend Easter sunrise with the vortex mystery.

I retraced my earlier steps and climbed a small hill until I reached the top. There the Mother Earth Vortex spread before me a mountain rim carved over eons, embracing a beautiful valley filled with pines, manzanita, sage and wildflowers.

As soon as my eyes were closed, the morning symphony of mountain birds began their overture to Easter.

On this wondrous morning, how grateful my heart was for the years of walking in the ranch wilderness. Those years had given me the confidence to come here today by myself. To walk into this wilderness with a sense of joyful connectedness. To sit on this hilltop stone feeling a sense of welcome belonging. Not a stranger to the awesome quality of wildness. Not afraid of seeing an order outside our human control.

The Mother Earth Vortex opened her beauty, sending my guide and teacher to give me information on how to proceed with my life, which was in answer to the question I had asked. Sitting quietly in meditation, this experience was given to me almost as though I were seeing myself in a motion picture.

Sedona Sunrise Easter morning, 1986.

The red rock mountains rise up around her as she enters the vortex known to Indians as the mystical home of the Earth Mother.

Small puffs of red rock dust swirl around her soft leather shoes as she walks quietly into the wide canyon.

Dew drops shine on pine branches. Touches of incredibly spring green leaves emerge out of brown branches.

A bird song reaches her. Another and another. A bird song symphony is played through the Boynton Canyon amphitheater, echoing back and echoing forward, a symphony filling the home of the Earth Mother, a welcoming sunrise.

She climbed up a small hill to sit on the top, engulfed by view. A deep breath as she settled atop a stone, perching herself just a few inches off the still damp ground.

With closed eyes and a mind that tried to be still, she sat, waiting.

Moonbeams. The word flashed across her inner eyelids. The taste of moonbeams. What is the taste of moonbeams?

The symphony comes to a crescendo. Suddenly there is a silence.

Do moonbeams taste the same way quicksilver looks? Are they cool and slippery?

Who is to say what moonbeams taste like? She smiled, thinking who would ask such a question, anyway?

"The heart asks those questions," a voice beside her said.

Normally she would have been startled and opened her eyes, but this early dawn Easter morning she did not.

"The heart knows the answer, too."

She did not have to open her eyes. She imagined clearly the voice speaking to her. It was the Indian guide with snakes tattooed on his arm. She had seen him before.

"Moonbeams taste like the joy of life, they are the luminescent ejaculation of joy—pure lifespirit—freely flowing—the coolness of mountain riverwater—moonbeams are."

"Will I ever know the taste of moonbeams?" she inquired.

"Your heart will ask again and find the answer for you."

She opened her eyes, sensing she was all alone.

It was true. She was alone with the symphony in the Vortex of the Earth Mother.

It was a test of faith. She would return again. She would ask again.

Perhaps one day she would be privileged to taste the moonbeams.

Hours had passed. Coffee in her styrofoam cup was cool.

She arose somewhat stiffly and stretched to begin the normal flow of blood once again.

Standing up, she was once more engulfed by the view. Brighter, sharper contrast now that the sun was far into the sky and long removed from the horizon.

It was necessary to disenthrall herself from this majestic, magnetic, electrifying place and continue back into the everyday.

Surely she would return. Surely she would inquire many times. Perhaps one day answers would also.

Moonbeams. The taste of moonbeams. The luminescent ejaculation of joy—pure lifespirit. Sedona!

Three hours passed as though only minutes. When the magical movie vision was over and my eyes opened, looking at the dirt at my feet, I saw there were patches of clay earth soaked with my own tears.

JOURNEY
INTO THE RUINS

AT THE DEPTHS of my despair about my ability to create a new life for myself, I felt as though I stood astraddle the chasm, the bottomless pit of nothing, of meaninglessness. My entire life had been built as a paper-thin crust across this chasm—and now it had crumbled. It was shattered into a thousand little pieces of sugar glass and disappeared into the dark chasm. There was no glimmer from its pieces, no trace of the flooring where a pit of blackness now yawned, pulling me into its mouth.

Suddenly, the ancient seduction of another forgotten darkness melted into this sucking mouth of destruction. Something I couldn't remember tugged and pulled at me, unbalancing my stance astraddle the chasm.

What was it, the haunting, the aching, the brush of shadow, across the peripheral vision of my own past? What was it that so unbalanced me now? What shadowed demon possessed the well-being of my life, haunting and hunting and ruining?

Why weren't there words? Damn it, there should be

words. It's not fair for there to be no words, no handles, no hands with which to reach out for help. Help. No words equal. No handles to hold onto, to brace yourself against the fall, to catch, to clutch, to grasp, to hold. No words equal, no handles with which to understand, to communicate, to validate. No parking, no standing, no being.

Without words there is no forgiveness. We're stuck with the shame of muteness, the mutiny of muteness. We rebel against ourselves. Without words, we cannot seek justice. There is no trial that anyone else can see, can share, can hear—because we have no words.

Damn it, there should be words. That's *not* fair. That's not just. Without words there will be no justice.

And so it is inevitable to think about death.

Or rather, I think about my inability to live, my inability to be alive. I don't know how to live my life. I don't know what to do. Who the hell am I anyway?

Who am I? If you take away what I have *done,* I cannot answer that question.

Who am I? Can I find a way to care about me if everything I have accomplished is stripped away from me? Can I care about my own naked, vulnerable self?

I don't know if I can. Maybe I don't know who she is. How can you be forty-six years old and not know who you are?

Maybe I never knew who I was. Maybe I never had time to spend knowing who I was. My life as a child was spent concentrating on saving myself from a crazy person.

The problem is how I feel so stupid. I feel like such a cliché.

My husband leaves me after nine years, with $250,000 of debt and taxes. A quarter of a million dollars of debt and no money left from everything I made before my illness. All gone.

Such a cliché, and the worst of it is the helplessness, the immobility.

How could I have reached out to save myself if I didn't even know the woman I was trying to save? Where did she come from?

Who is this creature with the cool, hurt, green eyes? Where did I lose touch with her? When did I cease to care about her? Why did I allow harm to come to her?

The sense of loss and grief are mountainous ruins in my path. No matter which way I choose each day, the circuitous route brings me before them.

We are not friends, this creature and I. Loss and grief have been denied entry and therefore they haunt rather than habitate. Habitating, they could eventually leave. Haunting, they are always felt. Haunting then, howling now, loss and grief are determined I shall make their ultimate acquaintance. This is now; there is no choice. I shall know them or I shall choose death. There is no way around the ruins of the past. They stand equally by, across the paths to the future. Ruins and ruins. They do not move. Eons standing, eons standing still. Ruins are ruins.

My ruins have made rooms. Hieroglyphs marked stories I could not read. Paths lead down corridors I cannot remember.

Panic. Why enter now? Why be forced into the ruins *now*? Why not run away? Run away. Get into the car and never come back. Let someone else handle the mountain of shit. Give someone else the responsibility.

The ruins stand quietly. No reproaches. No blame. They just stand in the way. They block the path totally. There is no alternate route.

And I who have *always* fought, that "me" of the eternal battle, the champion of "causes," defender of others' rights, I who have fought battles all my life, cannot now lift one finger to save myself. I look upon the struggle for my own survival with a dispassionate pain of acknowledgement, a knowing that no more battles can be waged until and unless the loss and the grief are accorded an honorable space. They are part of my equation: vulnerability equals annihilation. Loss and grief are the equal signs themselves. They are. And I am part of them. And they are a portion, a vast portion of the ruins. Perhaps they are the entrance, perhaps the gate. Maybe they are the exit as well. But—they are. Now, they must be acknowledged.

How? Tears are only a beginning. Loss and grief are not as easy as sorrow, sadness. Different than dying or death.

Dying and death in real life have ritual. Every culture has death ritual. Needs to needs, time and ritual.

Loss and feelings of grief have lost their ritual in our modern techno-dot plasticity. We left them behind in some measured progressiveness as culture shock. There is no yuppie/high-tech/fast lane room anymore for the ritual of loss and grief. No honor for them.

So each of us will encounter the phenomena of our own ruins in our own time, without benefit of ritual to cope, and we will stand as I will stand. I am at the ruins myself now.

The battle is temporarily gone; it is not over. There is no won-and-lost column tallied. Maybe there is no winning the battle in question. Maybe losing is just the passing of death over the scorecard. The battle continues on another playing field beyond our vision.

But today, it is not the sound of battle, not the stench of war, the sweat, the stench of sweat and war of fear, of words.

The ruins stand quiet, no reproach, no blame.

What do I do? How do I approach? What will happen to me? Who is it that enters, who will exit, who will exist?

Where will I find the little green-eyed girl? Is she really in there, waiting for me? Why do my eyes now fill with tears, my throat close so tightly, my breathing seem unnatural? What does that mean, to seek her, to find her? Why do I ache and cry—why?

Afternoon sun in my garden betrays no trace of the ruins, nor that I stand before them. The birds—real birds—sing, I hear breezes, faint noise of cars and a dog barking. That is one reality.

The faces of roses turned upward toward the sun, showing off in their radiance of many colors, show no signs of fear that the ruins are in their shared midst as they continue being roses, beautiful silver blue fragrance. Another reality.

Only I stand before the ruins with trepidation. Only I do not understand the naturalness with which they have appeared in my life, as my life, because of my life. Yet another reality. This is my reality.

And in the quiet void I stand knowing the unknown with no words that the ruins hold for me.

Despair.

I have a value structure which does not permit suicide. It is an amalgamation of religious beliefs, metaphysical principles and a firm conviction that reincarnation is the one general system that makes sense.

One set of ideas neither precludes nor supercedes the others. Rather, they exist in harmony as the puzzle pieces of my own spiritual quest, which began as a young girl with an abiding sense that God was with me. The journey has proceeded in fits and starts. Sometimes set aside, other times the major thrust of my preoccupation, always in different forms with various principles positioned in the foreground.

All of the ideas, the principles, individual values form a consensus structure, a system of thinking about life and the world that now precludes the choice of suicide as an alternative to dealing with pain.

Knowing, beyond my ability to verbalize it logically or for the benefit of other's ears, that I will not commit suicide, I am left with unacceptable choices, given that I have at this moment no earthly idea of how I am to proceed with living my life.

The problem is—nothing makes any sense to me. Why was I brought back to life after the stroke only to lose everything else in my life, everything I'd worked for, dreamed of, fantasized about. The future, as I had come to envision it, had been peeled away, stripped clean, made invisible to me. And I appear to be powerless to stop the course, to alter the events. Day after day, the movie of my life unfolds and my eyes are but spectators to witness the scene.

Strange. Very strange. This person, who all through the past has been so competent, now stands on the sidelines as the impassive witness to destruction. The spectator watching as a lifestyle sinks below the horizon.

Despair.

When my strength returns, the time for cleaning out the garbage begins. A process nauseating, filled with the pain of failure and the tragedy of not learning lessons set before your face.

The nausea is limited to four trash cans a week. I refuse to buy more receptacles for garbage. There is a limit to each soul's ability to cope with the putrid. It is therefore a slow process to clean out the residue of a nine-year marriage, a forty-six-year life. A slow and painful process, because this time, this part of my life must lay claim to the pain and the garbage before taking full responsibility for throwing it away.

Part of the problem has been my own disenfranchisement. Nothing was ever mine. As a child I was not permitted to have sovereign possessions. Nothing was ever mine. Toys, clothes, personal items were on temporary assignment. I did not decide when they would come in and when they were finished being used and could go out. Someone else, someone separate from me made those decisions and never told me why, or when. One day, without prior discussion or warning, my clothes or dolls or books or dog, or mother, father, brother, friend, school or whatever was designated as "Christina's" was *gone*. No explanation. No apology. No concern that it was a loss for me. No appreciation for my loss, my caring about those people or objects. And if I cried or screamed or sank into despair, I was punished for being ungrateful, I was chastised for being selfish. I was reprimanded for being unwilling to share. I was "wrong." I was disenfranchised totally, over and over and over again.

Taking away everything I cared about did not teach me to share, it taught me to hate. It did not teach me gratitude, it taught me dissociation. It did not teach me love, it taught me nothing but isolation. Later, I added self-punishment.

And now, once again, my body and soul stand before the entrance to the ruins. The green-eyed, silver-haired child.

I wonder if she has heard my tears across the forty years I have wandered from her.

Is it possible to find her again after all this time? Will she have waited?

Where are the tears for you, my sweet innocent? Who cried for you?

My sweet innocent, green-eyed, silver-haired child, innocent before the abandonment, before the seduction, the torture, the rape and the cruelty. Innocent before those emerald eyes caught sight of the indecent exposure, the lurid laughter, the putrid flesh stinking or ravenous hatred in the masquerade of sexuality and the rancid expressions of love.

My sweet innocent, even I abandoned you, terrified that you would perish in my own vulnerability. I left you behind, ever longing for your innocence, your playful touch, your sweet face trusting so completely, your softness and the crystal bell of your child's hearty laughter.

A thousand million times I have said "I'm sorry," yet never to you. The faces of my shame and sorrow show to others, but not to you.

I fought for a million children the world over, I pleaded and begged, I ranted and raved on their behalf—but not one word for you, my sweet innocent.

My God, have you waited all these years for my return? Have you trusted I would come for you, to make you a part of me, to bring you home at last?

I can hardly believe the tears which now fall so freely. They tell me I am coming home with my child, abandoned so long ago, left to dwell alone in the ruins.

Where were the tears for you, my sweet innocent? Who mourned for the emerald-eyed child buried alive in the ruins? Not I.

Leaving it all behind, I ran, I stumbled and scrambled and screamed and clawed my way out along the perimeter edge of the world, afraid of heights, afraid of deaths, afraid of closeness, afraid of darkness—afraid of life.

Who mourned your abandonment, my sweet innocent? Who wept over your seduction? Who comforted your wounded body after they tortured you? Who battled for your young life when you attempted teenage suicide? Who came to your defense when someone tried to murder you? Who howled with rage when the savages laughed and then tried to discredit you? Who mourned your virginity after the rape? NO ONE. NOT EVEN I.

And still...you waited? Is it true...you waited? Is it possible I can ever find you again, touch you, hold you, comfort you, caress the softness of you, make you smile, kiss your sweet face?

The agony of grief at the thought you might have vanished forever—is incomprehensible.

If I can weep for you, perhaps I can at last save myself.

Untold nights alone, frozen in fear of death. Then, irony of irony, untold days frozen in fear of life!

Why is it I chose to mutilate what's left when they finished the childhood torture? Is it that one has to learn early that care and compassion for one's frailty are necessary for survival, that failing to value, to learn kindness toward oneself only furthers the destruction?

One cannot learn compassion from those who rage. One cannot learn to nurture from those who destroy. One cannot learn love from those who value only power.

It is time to enter the ruins themselves, to be content to stand at their entrance.

What fantasy do I have that the ruins will yield an answer? What possible folly is it to dream that the ruins will point the direction for the journey to continue?

The walls of these ruins were lighter, rougher than in my imagination. The paths were wider, somewhat easier. My ears can discern the sound of crunching gravel as my feet begin the walk.

Will there be signs? How will I know which path to pursue?

The weather is calm, the sun overhead warm and bright, no discomfort, no danger.

Apparently I have been walking for some time.

Nowhere have I seen any clue as to whether or not I am on the right path.

I sit upon a small stone bench curved into or out from the stone wall. My eyes close in rest.

What is the purpose, I ask? What have I been sent to do? Why don't I know it, discover it? Where is the one to tell me?

"Do you believe in God?" The question came. I answered, "Yes," my eyes still closed.

"Do you believe you were sent to serve?" "Yes" I answered again.

"Then, is this a test of faith?" The question echoed through the ruins.

"A test of faith?" I asked. A test of faith. Nothing to hang onto, no sign, no life raft, no connection of right and wrong, no assurances, no direction. Despair. The dark night of the soul. A test of faith.

"I don't know," I answered.

"Is it possible?"

"Yes, it is possible."

All the old familiar doors have been closed. The way through them has been blocked. Everything that is past power has been taken away. Only enough energy to sustain. Only enough strength left for a small amount of time to take this journey.

Perhaps the universe is showing me that the doors I keep trying to open are not right for me now.

I realize they are closed. I have spent a lot of time and energy trying hard to open them. To no avail. They are closed and locked. Sealed imperviously to my efforts.

Yet with the full realization that they are *all* closed I plummet again into despair.

The universe is showing me that the path back into my old ways is blocked. All the routes are blocked. Unless I wish to keep pursuing useless avenues of dead ends, I must now recognize that I am not being permitted to retreat into the previously known. Nothing works there now for me.

Where then?

This is why I have been brought through my journey into despair—here, in the ruins. It is here I must dwell until the task of compassion is accomplished and until I retrieve what has been lost.

I know nothing about how to walk this past. My feet stumble on the path, incompetence, my own, is in my face. Only my strong hands seem capable. They remember through all the despair how to touch the earth, how to touch the heart of vibrations, how to soothe and how to be tender and how to grow. Perhaps I shall have to walk with my hands like the animals or the blind and not trust my feet only.

I open my eyes to see before me a woman whose face I may have known previously, yet today she is a stranger still.

Her voice is soft-spoken when she greets me. Her gentle nature is there with her.

"I am looking for a small person."

I said to her, not asking a question so much as sharing this part of my journey with her.

"She has silver hair and emerald eyes." Then I added, "She has been left here many years... maybe forty years, maybe thirty-five."

The gentle woman nodded her head, understanding.

"She has the gift of laughter. She has been wounded." Then I added in a whisper, "Have you seen her?"

"You are looking for a lost child?" Tears streaming down

my face as they have done each time I acknowledge my search for her, I answer, "Yes, I am looking for a child. I am searching for a lost child."

The tears cascade into weeping once again. My face is buried in my hands. My shoulders bear the burden of my sobs.

"Breathe," she says, quietly comforting me, with an arm cradling.

I have lost my will to live, been forced by the universe into this journey, now she tells me to breathe. It all sounds so simple. Breathe to live. Live to learn. Learn to serve. Have faith.

Unfortunately, it sounds to me like disaster and feels to me like despair. An empty cavern, a cavernous void. Nothing is out there—what will I do?

"Breathe," she says again. And I comply.

In a moment she begins to speak. At first it is hard to hear her words through tears. Fortunately she has time, and continues.

Slowly my tears have subsided. Her words ring clearly. She has opened a window through which I can see yet another view of that mystical energy called life.

"Thank you." Then through a deep breath, "I think you have just helped me save my own life."

The amber light that surrounded her shimmers in the coolness of the ruins. She smiles and, with a brief touch of her hand, is gone.

I still don't know where I'm supposed to go, but it doesn't seem so desperate a not-knowing. Perhaps I am to sit here, "not-knowing" until it is all right for me not to know what to do. Perhaps this also is another way to continuing. A painful, uncertain way that is uncomfortable for me.

But, painful or not, that is what it is. Is what is, what is...

a larger circle. Open up to what is. Open your heart up to what is you.

The crisis is transition. The crisis is not knowing. The crisis is believing, trusting, loving.

That is where you are. Open up to what is. Open your heart and the way will open too.

The night began. I fell asleep dreaming of the Earth Mother Canyon Vortex and remembering Sedona.

In my dream, the spirit guide of the Indian with two snakes tattooed on his arm appeared. I have yet to see his face. He is tall. I can see the snakes most clearly. They are a symbol whose meaning is not yet clear to me.

He begins by saying his name. White Owl Rising. He has been sent to me. He says, "The vortex is a place in your mind, once you have been there. You can come back any time and you will. You have chosen a very difficult journey, which is not over yet. There is more to come. *Do not despair.* We will keep you well enough to continue. I have been sent to you because you cared for us and the sacred places in the wilderness. They will lose the property because they do not respect it. Step out of the way and let it go. Millions depend on you. Your life lights the way. Your journey lights their way. You have important work to do in the prisons. Your book will be published. *Do not despair.* We will be with you."

I awoke to see the ground covered with my tears. Water was streaming down my face from my eyes. I made no attempt to stem the flow or stop the intense feeling with no name.

It was morning. In these ruins today, I thought, I shall find the child.

What will I say to her? How shall I explain this long journey back, to her, to us, to the me of my own future?

Even though there were still no signs, my feet seemed to

begin knowing which turn to take, which to avoid. The pace quickened and with it my heartbeat.

We were coming closer to her. My entire body told me that her presence was not far away.

Around one more corner and the path opened into a small courtyard filled with fragrant flowers and cool shade trees. To one side, facing me, stood the child.

My breath caught in my throat and the sight stopped my footsteps.

I stood very still, searching to discern whether she was real or if, in fact, she was just a statue, or perhaps another dream.

The child was about four feet tall with long silver-blond hair and crystal green eyes. She wore a plain dress with ribbons top and bottom and a sash tied around her tiny waist. Her skin was lightly touched by the color of the sun but pale and soft. In her hands she held a pale blue-violet rose, in her hair was a daisy chain garland.

We looked at one another across the courtyard and the thirty-five or forty intervening years.

I didn't know what to say, how to begin.

"I'm Christina," I offered.

"So am I," she replied.

"I've come a very long way and I'm so glad to have found you."

She said nothing, studying me with deepest eyes that looked as if they knew too much for the age she appeared to be which was somewhere between four and six years old.

"This is hard for me but I've come to ask forgiveness... I'm sorry. I didn't mean to abandon you. I thought it would hurt you more to take you with me because the journey was such a bitter one and I was so terrified."

"I missed you, always," she whispered.

Oh my God, I moaned, choking back the tears which fell anyway. I opened my arms and she ran to me seeking the safety and refuge I'd denied her over an entire lifetime.

Together we cried for all that was past. The terrors, the torture, the inner pain, the doubt, the self injury. The withdrawal from life itself. We held each other and wept for the lack of safety. The absence of love and trust. The years of shame.

"I need you to help me learn to play," I said softly. "Even in the bad times we used to have fun, make up wonderful games, visit with creatures from our imagination. I have forgotten how to play, because that was the price of leaving you behind."

"I know." She nodded sadly.

"You have the gift of laughter," I said to the child.

"You do too. Across the years I have heard it echo back, unmistakable."

We smiled at one another. It was true.

Her small hand held tightly to mine. It was extraordinary, seeing myself so soft and vulnerable, trusting and innocent.

I touched her fingers, pudgy still and without the length or strength of adulthood. There, in the center of each palm, right and left, between the parallel lines that ran horizontally the width of her hand, was a cross, like the letter X.

Then I looked at my own hands, matching hers. To my right hand time and life had added a second cross and many more lines, but the basic pattern was identical.

"Is there anything I could say to you that would be helpful?"

She looked very serious for a long minute. It reminded me of the way I still tended to withdraw into my own private world when someone outside of me became too close or too insightful.

Patiently, I waited for her response, knowing beyond mere words what she was feeling.

"Do you love me?" she asked, avoiding direct contact with my eyes.

"Yes, I love you very much. I didn't know that for a long time. I'm sorry."

"If you love me, why were you so ashamed of me? Why did you hide me? Why did you keep running away from me?"

The years of humiliation showed clearly on her small up-turned face. She had dark shadows under her eyes.

"I don't know. I was scared. I tried to act grown up, to be strong so they couldn't hurt me more."

"You are strong. I am strong. Maybe we don't have to worry about that one anymore." She smiled through the seriousness.

"Maybe," I said. "I didn't know much about loving, I guess. I knew only about needing. I have had a lot to learn about being a friend before I started on this journey to find you. All my life I found myself leaving, just as I left you, and then wondering why I never felt as though I belonged anywhere. There was a whole lifetime of mistakes to sort through and figure out before I got to the point that I knew I had to find you again. Then I became terribly frightened that you wouldn't be here after all these years, that I had lost you forever."

Her child's innocent face looked at me and smiled. "Didn't you know . . . Lost is a place, too! Can't you see? Lost is where both of us are right now."

Her crystal laughter broke through my solemnity, cutting away the trepidation, the hesitation, the shyness. That crystal sound grasped my heart, tugging at it to open and let her inside.

Embracing her with my arms and my heart, I joined in her laughter.

Of course—it was so simple. "Lost is a place, too." I should have know that. God knows I've spent enough time in my life there, in that place called Lost. How fitting that that is the place I should have been sent to look for her. That lost place in myself. That place I thought I had lost. The child I had abandoned and left behind for fear the rest of the journey would surely kill her.

Yet there she stood before me. She was a miracle filled with crystal laughter, looking at me through shining emerald eyes.

"I love you," she whispered.

Tears of joy mixed with untold years of anguish and despair instantly filled my eyes.

"My God, child . . . I love you too."

The grasp she had on my heart finally pried the stubborn door loose and inside she walked, my heart wide open to her for the first time in our lives.

Once again it was night. She slept safely, peacefully, quietly inside my heart all through the darkness.

It felt good to know she was nestled there, out of harm's way, loved and cared for by me. I was proud of the courage it had taken to come this far, of the despair that had brought me first to my knees and then to this journey.

She had wisdom and compassion of her own. She had strength and joy. She had laughter and mischief. She was shy and withdrawn too, but together we would resolve that pain from the past. She still had hope and could dream for the future. I would ask her to share her gifts with me.

Now I am able to protect her, to cherish her, to fight for her and win. I can teach her about patience, which she rarely had, and about love, which I am still learning.

Together we should be able to venture into trust more than we have in the past and combat the feeling of helplessness we both feel so often in the face of betrayal, disloyalty, cruelty and evil.

We're going to make a hell of a team, kid. No more loneliness, for either of us.

This is the last time anyone can disown us. First my birth mother disowned me. Then my adopted mother disowned me. Then I disowned you. No more. That's all gone. Over. No more.

We're continuing this journey, whatever it is, together.

When morning finally came, I asked the child if she would be comfortable remaining in my heart for the continuation of our journey. She giggled something about basically being a lazy soul, which was her way of saying "yes."

Together we said good-bye to that special place called Lost and began to find our way out of the ruins of the past.

THE INITIATE

THE DAY I walked out of the ruins, holding the child in my heart, was the beginning of a new life for me.

My journey into the ruins was to retrieve the lost pieces of my childhood spirit, those pieces of my soul without which I could never feel complete, without which I could not proceed.

Now that I had within me the lost component parts of myself, I could begin to build my new life.

How can I begin to explain what has happened next?

It seems to be a series of unconnected adventures.

I am a novice. I am learning, but I still don't know how to live this life without some old ideas, old values, old goals. However, I know I have to find an entirely new way.

The process is bizarre. "Listen to your inner voice, your intuition and go where it leads you." Those were the only instructions.

In the beginning when I was learning to listen for it, I was positive that my inner voice had a serious case of laryngitis! It was so faint I wondered sometimes if I were perhaps going deaf as well. If it was now my destiny to live as though I'd stepped off the edge and into the void, at least, in all fairness, I should have my hearing intact.

In our Western culture it is a different process for people to be initiated into the journey of the soul.

Many other cultures—particularly those in the Orient—do have such practices, rituals, rites of passage, initiations that are only loosely tied to everyday religion. Their individual journey of the soul is part of the process of spiritual development and is not necessarily recognized as secular religion, which, in Western culture, is partially political and culturally based.

Even the search itself is often discouraged. You are always faced with the following question: If searching for the true journey of your soul doesn't produce immediate, productive results, what good is it in a culture of materialistic instant gratification?

However, I also covered the part belonging to organized religion. In fact, I covered it first because it was what I understood best.

Years earlier, I had started to attend St. Nicholas, a beautiful old neighborhood Episcopal church in Encino that was built in the 1930s to resemble a small Spanish mission. The first time I went to St. Nicholas was for a friend's wedding. My next visit there was Christmas Eve midnight mass.

As a child I'd been brought up in Christian Science, so I'd never been baptized because that denomination has no rituals, no ministry, or ceremonial liturgy.

After my "membership" in AA was established, I called the rector of St. Nicholas and asked for a meeting with him regarding adult baptism.

Father Williams' office was lined floor to ceiling with books. I felt as though I'd stepped back in time to an English country village and the parish rectory at the turn of the century.

He asked about my family, my previous religious background. I told him about being adopted, about the Christian Science Church and the girls' Catholic convent where I'd graduated from high school.

In answer to his questions, I tried to explain my feeling of belonging at St. Nicholas, the need to be connected to tradition and ritual, the desire for communion. It was then he told me that St. Nicholas was known originally as the "Children's Church."

On September 21, 1984, the feast of Saint Matthew, the Reverend Evan R. Williams baptized me at ten o'clock in the morning near the church altar rail. The next Sunday I would take communion.

It was a wonderful feeling to take care of myself in this way. I didn't mind if nobody understood. I didn't feel the need to notify the world of what had happened.

It was disappointing that my husband was unable to be with me. Unfortunately he was on a long-distance business phone call and never showed up at the church.

But the baptism wasn't about my husband. The baptism was about my own soul.

Over the next year I attended church regularly, by myself. David began his long business trips just three months after my baptism.

I breathed a sigh of relief after the baptism. It was as though I'd put myself on the right course. Perhaps it was a bit like taking out spiritual insurance.

Now I waited for another signal.

Months passed as I watched my life take one turn after another for the worse.

A public offering for a business my husband and I initiated months earlier failed to sell out by the deadline, so I had to terminate it by myself and arrange for the money to be returned to all the investors.

There was no other choice now but to begin the process of cleaning up the mess left behind from what I now realized were years of poor business decisions and broken dreams.

David was in Chicago.

A GIFT
FOREVER

IN SEPTEMBER 1985 one of my articles for Redbook Magazine was being published. The magazine public-relations department arranged an interview for me on "Good Morning America," the same program I'd had so much trouble with before my stroke. I was delighted with the ability to return under such good circumstances. It made me feel as though I were beginning to turn the tide around to better times.

I flew to New York on Sunday a few days early and checked into the St. Moritz Hotel on Central Park South. The television show kept a VIP suite there for guests which consisted of two large rooms on the twentieth floor with a balcony overlooking Central Park. It was a beautiful setting. I was happy to be in New York, to be on the show, to have published the article and now to enjoy this suite of rooms with its magnificent view of the park. Sometimes everything in your life looks just right. You get a glimpse of how it could be all the time. It's an exhilarating experience.

Part of my anticipation had nothing to do with work. Part of the excitement was purely personal.

Nine years of marriage and total fidelity to my husband was at an end. I realized my life now required me to reach out beyond that relationship and seek companionship elsewhere. But where to begin?

A month ago I'd been in the city for one day, also on business, and called a lifelong friend to see if we could meet for dinner.

Sitting with him, the years we'd shared in the past, both as friends and as previous lovers, came flowing back into my memory. He'd never married and I teased him about only being attracted to unavailable women, which seemed true to me.

As that evening progressed, a thought occurred to me that needed time to develop.

We laughed and talked about mutual friends. I'd known this man since I was seventeen years old. We'd shared dreams and secrets. We'd worked together, helped each other. We'd been friends sometimes, lovers other times, and there was a deep, wordless bond between us even now.

The experience of seeing him, talking with him, felt as though I were reconnecting broken fragments of myself, felt like the best of visits with family, where you silently acknowledge the strong ties going way back into the past, unbroken because the memory exists even if you haven't thought about them in years.

When I returned to California, his face, his voice echoed constantly through my mind. Being with him was not like being with a new person. Even though we hadn't seen one another in many years, he was familiar. He knew me when most of the current people in my world hadn't. He knew my struggles, my weaknesses. He admired my talent and always professed to love me.

Twenty years before, we'd been together off and on in

both New York and Los Angeles. Even then he didn't want to be tied down, wanted to be free to play the field—and did. Every time we'd become really close, he'd become unavailable or leave. It made me crazy because of all my old bullshit about abandonment. Fortunately, long after we agreed not to continue as lovers we were still good friends.

And now with a large part of both our lives gone by, here we were again, face-to-face, thinking about being lovers again.

So in September, feeling well nurtured by my recent work, which provided this unexpected trip, I was willing to take a chance with him, see where it went, how I felt.

He picked me up at the airport and we spent all day Sunday alone together in the country less than an hour from New York City, walking in the woods, sitting and talking on a quiet rocky beach.

There were years of events and feelings and transitions and changes to catch up with in one another's lives.

In addition there was a secret consideration of mine that I couldn't even find courage to voice.

Although by now I was fully recovered from my stroke, the right side of my entire body, head to toe, still had diminished physical sensation. It was the last minor vestige of the paralysis that had originally been quite severe.

Under ordinary circumstances, the condition didn't bother me at all. It now seemed "normal" for me, and whatever compensations were needed, I'd already made.

However, the physical activity of making love was different. And that's where my extreme shyness was now surfacing.

Since my illness, my husband and I had not been physically very attracted to one another. To all intents and purposes, I hadn't been with anyone else in almost a year and not been with anyone but my (now estranged) husband for over ten years.

Between my illness and my fidelity, which had turned into celibacy, I was concerned that I wouldn't remember how to be a lover. What if I really didn't feel the physical sensations anymore? What if that was just one more consequence of the life changes I had to accept?

My mind was in the midst of this turmoil as we drove back to his New York apartment late in the afternoon. Excitement and nervousness alternated like electric currents. I felt like a high-school girl, not a mature woman.

What amused me somewhat was the fact that before I met David and got married, I'd had lots of dates and lots of lovers. In a total transition, I'd made the vow of fidelity to my husband and never regretted one minute of it.

Now, however, in this new phase of my life, I felt so vulnerable and inept. I just couldn't seem to recall the slick and provocative behavior that used to come so easily to me in the years of my twenties and early thirties.

Fortunately my friend and lover sensed part of what I was feeling and made transitions easier for me.

We had been here before, not in this apartment, but as lovers. I recognized his kiss, his touch on my skin.

Lying naked on his big antique bed, surrounded by soft quilts, fluffy pillows, listening to quiet jazz music and seeing his face in the candlelight, I felt with amazement the sensuous reconnection with my own femininity.

Tears of sheer joy streamed down my face. My body was alive again—all of my body was alive again! I didn't have to accept the sadness of not feeling like a woman, the loss of sexuality, the shame of being unattractive in the deepest, most fundamental sense.

Over the next five or six hours, as we made love and

talked and made love again, he gave me a great gift for which I am eternally grateful. I had thought that sensuality had gone from my life forever.

To be reconnected to myself, to my innermost passion, to be free to express those feelings in trust and love was an astonishing experience for me.

He is an accomplished and creative lover. He is strong and romantic at the same time. He is also a person of passion and never withdrew from me when we were on the edge of falling into chaos.

Wherever he is in this world, my love goes with him forever. We are not able to be together anymore for a variety of reasons, but it doesn't diminish what we shared, what I learned. It will never diminish the gift he gave me nor the joy I feel, knowing I am complete and whole once again, which has nothing whatsoever to do with having an ongoing relationship with him. A gift given is a gift forever.

It was wonderful risk-taking for both of us. He had to face his long-held fantasy of being in love with me and I had to find the courage to be vulnerable. It was a good experience for both of us.

In addition to reclaiming my child spirit from the ruins, I now renewed my sense of pride in being a woman, whole and beautiful.

The incredible burden of my entire past began to lift, to lighten, to shift and dissolve.

THE KEYS ARE
IN THE GARBAGE

DURING MAY AND June 1986 my life was busy with commission work for the Department of Children's Services and Dependency Court, with initial preparations for the play I was producing in the fall, and with speaking engagements which took me to the East and Midwest.

The next step of my spiritual journey brought me back to Dick Sutphen. I had been searching for nonpsychotherapeutic methods of healing at this time in my life because psychotherapy didn't address the issue of our connection to the universe, a vitally important issue to me now. Sutphen's approach seemed to be exactly what I wanted.

One week, the end of July, I spent in Dick Sutphen's Bushido training at the new organization headquarters in Agoura, California. It was a fantastic five days. The group was about thirty-five people from all over the country.

What we were learning was a way of accessing the information stored in ourselves. We then used that retrieval process to make progress through previous stumbling blocks of our own consciousness.

Some dramatic material came up for most of the participants in the past life regression segments.

We learned daily how to take ownership of ourselves, our lives, past and present, how to release resentment and how to see patterns in our karmic pathways.

I learned that each of us is absolutely responsible for the quality of our own life. I alone am responsible for all the choices that construct the quality of my life. My choices are the thoughts I think to myself about everything and everyone in my world. My choices are aspirations and fears, expectations and assumptions.

During these few intense days, I learned that by going back into the past, beyond this present life, I could see my relationship with my mother more clearly—that it had taken many twists and turns as we had played out our mutual destinies, fulfilling our individual growth toward enlightenment. Each lifetime, we had chosen very difficult circumstances and this lifetime had not changed that pattern. The difference was that now I was finally beginning to comprehend the meaning of it and to have compassion for each of us.

Immediately after this intensive workshop I flew up to Berkeley for a weekend seminar with Michael Harner, the anthropologist who teaches an ancient spiritual development and healing process.

This was my vacation, my gift to myself.

Since none of my old habits, old ways of living life had worked, I was learning to explore new ones.

In order to pursue these ideas, it was necessary to pay very close attention to what seemed to spark my interest, to follow every clue. Perhaps most importantly, I had to discover a safe place for me to live in the universe. I had to find a way of connecting to power that makes safe places,

places of nurturance. Finding that place and connecting with that power meant a fundamental shift from seeing the world as a place of war and punishment to seeing the world as a place of life and fulfillment.

As a member of the Institute of Noetic Sciences for the last few years, I had received its quarterly journal and research papers. In one of the journals there had been an interview with Michael Harner and his work on shamanism. I wrote to the Foundation for Shamanic Studies in Norwalk, Connecticut, for information on Dr. Harner's upcoming workshops.

Shamanism has been confused in Western minds with witch doctors. The way of shamanism is, in fact, a most ancient and reliable method of spiritual healing and information gathering from cosmic consciousness for the benefit of not only the individual but also the community.

Michael Harner himself is a bear of a man dressed in blue workshirt and jeans, with thick glasses, a grey beard, a mischievous sense of humor and a great strength of being.

On the second day of the workshop Michael and I had lunch together at a famous old Berkeley hangout called Brennans, a huge place dominated by an oval bar. Along one wall is a cafeteria line with steam-table food and mammoth sandwiches, which are made to order.

The bar is run by the Irish and the kitchen by the Chinese, which always appealed to Michael's anthropological curiosity.

I sat across from this man, watching him eat his meal while I drank tea. Three or four television sets mounted on stands hanging from the ceiling were blaring on different channels. I could hardly believe that yesterday he'd been a stranger to me, not that we were close friends now. We were only brief acquaintances to one another. Rather I had an intuition that here was another human being with whom I could share information about this very strange journey I found myself living. He made it clear to me that experiences such as mine were often an integral part of the calling to spiritual work.

In this other world, the world he'd been initiated into by South American Indians, it was all perfectly normal. Yes. There was another reality. Ordinary reality was not the only dimension available to us. Nonordinary reality was also accessible, without drugs, without hypnosis, without the sleeping dreamstate.

The path to nonordinary reality, its teachers and its treasurehouse of sacred information is what Michael taught. It was not just simply a matter of understanding. It consisted of sets of skills and processes, requiring willingness, diligence, practice and wisdom.

What a phenomenal experience. Finally the doors were unlocking. World after world was opening up to me.

And to think how long I'd been stuck in my place called Lost!

As my plane took me back to Burbank Airport, I read Michael's book, *The Way of the Shaman,* and wondered how many others knew any of the information. It was fascinating to look at these total strangers in the airplane and try to guess how much they may have seen, what they might know.

The following Monday morning I had appointments booked solid for both the play I was producing and other business.

After showering, dressing and making several phone calls it was time to leave. But, the car keys were not where I usually put them in my purse. Strange.

The car keys were not on my dresser, not in the pocket of

my jacket from yesterday, not in the kitchen and not on my desk.

By now, I was getting annoyed. They had to be in the house somewhere because my car was sitting in its usual place in the driveway.

Unfortunately, there was no second set of car keys. They had disappeared some time ago and not been replaced.

There was nothing left to do but call several friends to see if they could help me out and then call the Cadillac dealer where the car was originally purchased and ask for new keys to be made.

At 10:30 I finally left my house for the string of meetings, got back to the car dealership at four that afternoon and arrived home at 4:45 p.m.

When I went out to start my car, the new keys didn't fit!

A friend had come by to swim and instead of cooling off in the pool we dashed back to the car dealership to have them make a second set of new keys. They had just closed when we arrived but I went through the showroom and into the back garage to plead with the guy for another try at new keys.

He obviously saw my desperate face and took pity, quickly making the two additional keys.

It must have been one hundred and ten degrees in the San Fernando Valley that day and neither of my friend's cars had air-conditioning.

I was hot and sweaty and aggravated. When we arrived back home, the first thing I did was try the new key in the car ignition.

The damn key still did *not* fit!

I couldn't believe it. I stared at this useless key in total dismay. What the hell was going on?

I took a deep breath, trying to catch hold of my temper

before it blew. What good is metaphysics, I thought, when the damn car keys don't fit.

After a minute I decided that the only possible thing to do right now was to go swimming. I needed to cool off and calm down.

After all, I had just spent the last seven days going through intensive training on learning how to access all the information I needed to live my life successfully without anger! I had just spent seven days learning that:

The answers are within.

The irony about this whole business was that I'd managed to lose my car keys in my own house. That meant they had to be here. But where? Obviously, they were presently in "Lost." Even though I understood that Lost is a place, I still could not find my car keys.

It struck me as an even greater irony that this experience was a metaphor for my experience of the past few years.

Even while swimming, I could not keep that thought from recurring, that the lost keys were a metaphor for this whole time of my life. Not only that, but I lost them in my own house!

Going outside doesn't help either. Outside keys don't work!

I felt like a real lunatic *knowing* that I had somehow thrown the keys away to teach myself a lesson. Immediately after spending seven days learning how to go within, learning that each of us have all our own answers, learning that we have unlimited power to create our own realities and that we *choose* everything, I came home and misplaced my car keys. This present situation is not a coincidence. There are no accidents.

I keep telling myself, this business with the car keys is no coincidence, even though it makes me feel as though I'm going bananas, as if I have completely stepped over the edge. This is a lesson in consciousness.

Without my car keys, I am stuck. I cannot go anywhere. Losing my keys is now a very expensive mistake. Calling a locksmith to come out to the house and make me keys would cost a fortune.

I knew this was a lesson about trusting myself, a lesson about listening to my intuition, a lesson about being able to hear my inner voice when it speaks to me.

Swimming laps of the pool, I quieted my mind and concentrated on the resulting emptiness until I calmed down. Then as I got out of the pool and walked toward the chair where my towel lay, an intuitive flash came to me.

"The keys are in the garbage" was the information just as clearly spoken as if someone had been standing next to me.

It stopped me cold. I stood in my tracks, dripping wet.

"The keys are in the garbage?" I blurted out loud.

My friend was still swimming in the pool.

"What did you say?" she asked nonchalantly.

"I think I know where the keys are," I mumbled.

"Well, that's good!" she replied cheerfully.

After drying myself hurriedly I went into the house to think.

Decision: do I follow the intuition and look through all the garbage cans? Do I risk feeling very foolish if the keys are not there after all?

Okay—do I *not* follow the intuition but just dismiss it and take the penalty by calling the locksmith?

It took almost one hour to get up the courage to follow my intuition. Part of my problem was the thought of following this "inner voice" into the garbage. What made me crazy was the thought of the terrible mess and feelings of humiliation if it were all a cosmic joke just to see how gullible I was.

Why couldn't I have been told that my keys were in the laundry or the refrigerator, or almost anywhere else but the garbage?

Now. What was I going to tell my friend? Was I actually going to say that a *voice* told me that my keys were in the garbage? That's good, I thought, for sure I'll never see her again. After all, what person wants a friend who hears voices telling her to go rummaging around through garbage cans in hundred-degree heat? But, if I don't say anything and she just finds me with my head in the garbage can, she's going to think I'm cracked anyway. So I think I'm trapped, no matter which way I choose.

I decided to tell her and take my chances. I now seriously wondered if my inner voice was some kind of cosmic prankster. If so, this cosmic prankster must be getting one whopping good laugh today!

My friend followed me outside. I took a deep breath and started taking garbage out of one of the four cans that I thought might be the right one.

Piece by piece I emptied the contents of the bags.

About halfway down, between empty cat food cans, dead lettuce and avocado peels, I actually *saw* the car keys!

I let out a whoop and a holler the whole neighborhood could hear, grabbed onto the keys, and jumped into the air in total exhilaration.

Laughing and crying at the same time I embraced my friend in joyous triumph. No words came to me, only sounds of victory.

I was shaken by the power of the affirmation of the intuition, by the power of the demonstration, by the power of this lesson from the universe in the real world, in real time and real life! *The keys are in the garbage!*

The power swept over me.

We really do have all our own answers. We *can* find our way with those answers. It is a power from the universe we are all given. It is intended to be used and honored. Even our own garbage can teach us valuable lessons!

Yesterday, in the workshop journey process Michael taught us, I had asked my spiritual teacher in nonordinary reality a question and the teacher had replied.

"Take off your head if you want to proceed on your journey. Validate your intuition, for it serves you very well. The information you seek is within you now. You have magic. Through time and space that is what is true. That is what will serve you. That is what you must follow. It is leading you now. You must take hold of all the information that comes. It is important. It will lead you. Do not discount anything you're told, no matter how bizarre it seems at first. It is your journey. Be aware that it may not be what you are used to but do not be uncomfortable with it. You will lead others to see their journey. It is." This information was a validation of the beginning of my ability to become connected to the universe.

So, the truth is: I had put the car keys in my own garbage and then . . . I said the car keys were *LOST!*

I laughed and laughed and laughed.

HONORING
THE DAUGHTER

PRODUCING CRAIG CHILDRESS' play, *Animal Games*, during the fall of 1986 was a milestone.

Since my stroke five years earlier I had done major speaking engagements, written feature magazine articles for TV Guide, Ladies' Home Journal and Redbook magazines, founded a grass-roots non-profit Survivors Network for adults who were abused as children, and served a Los Angeles County Commissioner for Children's Services. Yet, I did not have a full-time job.

Frankly, the play was a challenge because I didn't know whether or not I had the physical stamina to work such long hours under pressure. It was something I had not tackled until now.

Craig's play was special and unusual. As a writer he chose to explore current social issues such as alienation, pain, sexual abuse, but he also engaged you in the characters before you knew about their problems. He created a special comedy-drama style for his play that I liked.

Having spent fourteen years in theater myself, I particularly looked forward to putting that experience to work again, this time not as an actress but as a producer.

I'd decided to produce the play at the Lee Strasberg Creative Center theater on Santa Monica Boulevard in West Hollywood under the Equity Waiver rules, Los Angeles' answer to Off-Off Broadway in New York.

The theater sat only ninety-nine people but every seat had a good view.

After four weeks of rehearsal we opened in October to mixed reviews and ran for eight weeks. The cast of four actors was fabulously talented. Peter DeLuise, who played the lead character and wore a chicken suit for most of the two acts, won a Drama Logue critics' award for his outstanding performance.

After the closing I drove up to visit my stepfather, Phillip Terry, and his wife, Roz, who lived in Montecito.

Phillip and Roz had come down to Los Angeles for the opening but I hadn't been up to visit them in the two months since.

We had a lovely lunch at the country club, talked about future plans for the play, which they'd enjoyed, and gossiped about current events in their world.

Phillip had only been married to my adopted mother for three years, from the time I was about three until I was six. Yet, when I came back to California at twenty-one as a young actress under contract to 20th Century-Fox Studios, Phillip had contacted me and we'd been in touch with one another off and on ever since.

However, in the last five or six years, we'd seen more of one another and recently he'd not been feeling well so I tried to visit on a more regular basis. Roz always made me feel like a member of the family. I'd grown to love her too.

Today in addition to the usual banter at the time of my

departure, Phillip had been more verbal about how deeply he cared for me, calling me his daughter and saying that with Roz, I was the only family he had left.

I was deeply touched as I hugged them both good-bye.

Tears were still in my eyes as I drove through the country-side toward the Pacific Coast Highway. As I rode down the beautiful coastline, seeing the groups of young surfers, an ocean of whitecaps, sailboats, and faint outlines of the Santa Barbara Channel Islands, I was filled with a sense of happi-ness and feelings of belonging.

Why was it that before now I'd never really allowed my-self to feel close to my stepfather? He'd always been kind to me, always stayed in touch with me, always made me feel welcome.

Suddenly another flash of understanding hit me like a lightning bolt. Tears streamed down my face again making it nearly impossible for me to continue driving.

More giant puzzle pieces of my life suddenly shifted and fell into place. I could see it all so clearly. It all made so much sense.

Phillip left our house when I was about six years old. Be-cause of the circumstances, the departure was abrupt.

One day he was there. The next day when I came home from school, he was gone.

All trace of him vanished also. All his things were gone, the dresser and closet in his room were empty. All the pho-tographs of him around the house were gone. And, in our family albums the photographs with him had been ripped, removing his image.

No one seemed to know what happened or where he went. He was the only father I'd ever known. I was devas-tated.

But today, I understood the whole past dilemma.

SURVIVOR

As a little girl, I realized I was both terrified and angered by his departure. He left me all alone in that house and never said good-bye. My feeling of loss and grief overwhelmed me. There was no one to comfort me, no one with whom to share my pain, no one who could explain things to me.

It seemed reasonable to me, at that age, never to put myself through that much pain again. So, when he reappeared sixteen years later, I was polite and casually responsive but wouldn't let him into my inner world.

However, by shutting out my stepfather when I was six years old, I also shut out other people, other important feelings like trust and love.

I don't think I ever really trusted anyone again.

I don't think I ever felt attracted to anyone as either a friend or later as a lover without a deep, gnawing feeling that they, too, would be taken away from me for reasons I wouldn't understand. I then formulated a dreadful bargain with people in my life. The bargain dictated "If you love me, I'll take care of you." That bargain came from the little-girl time of my life. It was what I always wanted someone to say to me.

At no time in my growing up years did I feel secure in my world. It was as though I lived on an earthquake fault that quivered and shook without warning.

Understanding what I must have felt as a child when I lost my father allowed me now to release all of it. This deep understanding now allowed me to release the hurt, the pain, the fear and the rage. It allowed me to feel love for Phillip and accept his offer to be family.

Tears still streamed down my face as I drove through the early winter afternoon.

What a fabulous gift to have just received. The gift of understanding.

It's true. The giant puzzle pieces are now all fitting together.

I have brought the child with me in my heart, taken her out of the ruins called Lost and reenfranchised her in my life. I have set her free. Now I have reclaimed the daughter and honored the adult woman I am. Today, I have set myself free from the unconscious patterns based on childhood pain.

I don't have to feel enraged over this ever again. The anger is gone because the fear of loss that fuels it is also gone.

How wonderful that Phillip and I both lived to see this day. We have both learned lessons on the journey. I have learned this lesson of love and belonging. I have come to belong to this part of myself, to love and honor the daughter. I have a father—my stepfather—the person sent by the universe, the one I chose to learn this lesson with and through.

The feeling was one of great joyous connection to life and to the process of being alive. I was now forty-seven years old. Phillip was almost eighty. It had taken me nearly forty-one of my years to get this part straightened out, free from the struggle, shifted over from hurt and fear to love.

Now that I understand the nature of my feelings of grief, the real trauma and loss and fear and anger I felt, I can also appreciate what my adopted mother must have gone through.

Now, I don't have to worry about trying to take care of everyone because I'm so afraid of them disappearing if I don't.

Now I can find out about new ways of relating to others

while allowing them to be who they are. And, if they leave, it's because they choose to, not because of something within me.

The journey has taken most of a lifetime for each of us, but perhaps that's the real purpose of lifetimes.

THE SPIRITS
OF THE PLACE

THERE'S AN UNOBTRUSIVE street that joins Benedict Canyon and winds upward, narrowing as it ascends until there is only enough room for one car.

About halfway up is the address where a woman purported to have studied American Indian medicine lives. The address is in the Beverly Hills postal area but the atmosphere resembles a small country canyon village.

She greets me at the front door looking very much like photographs I'd seen of her. A pretty, diminutive woman, she has hair consisting of masses of silken ringlets which surround her face. She wears colors well, seeming to attract them to her rather than simply putting them on.

We talk rather casually as she ritually smudges me, symbolically cleanses me with smoke and feather.

For a few minutes we sit in her living room, which is filled with American Indian artifacts. She asks me a few questions about myself, how I'd come to her and what I wanted.

This visit is an early birthday present, as it is the end of April and my birthday isn't until June. What I need from this woman is spiritual information on how to protect myself from people who were trying to hurt me.

For months I'd been involved in futile attempts to sell the ranch and to settle the business affairs left over from my marriage and the divorce.

Progress kept being delayed, the struggle continued and it was deeply frustrating. Once again, only the various lawyers were getting anything good out of the mess.

The woman tells me to write down a process she is going to give me and tells me to perform the ritual ceremony by myself in the wilderness.

For the next half hour I write furiously on the large yellow legal pad, trying to set down every detail she says. It will be important to follow the order in which she gives me the information and to remember all the various pieces of the ritual.

The hour passes with lightning speed. She walks me to the door and hugs me good-bye. I take a deep breath and step back into the spring afternoon sunlight.

During the next few weeks I have work to do for the commission and several speaking engagements in other states.

Several times I recopy the details I had been given and make a list of the items needed for the ceremony.

The first free day I have, I drive north with my two large dogs and my friend who'd shared the great day of insight when I found my car keys in the garbage can. She had already experienced some of the events with me that this journey was carrying me through and I thought it better not to go through the long drive all alone, even if she could not stay with me during the time I was doing the ceremony.

There was a place I knew, a place where Indians had been, where the medicine wheel I was to make would be safe and could be left intact. We could only drive part way on a dirt road that joined the paved highway in what otherwise seemed to be country in the middle of nowhere.

We leave the car in the shade under a large oak tree and walk up further into the mountain wilderness on foot.

The dogs are ecstatic to be running free again as they had done for their first three years of life on the ranch. They would disappear for a while and then pop out of the chaparral brush, hundreds of yards further along. So far, they have never run away.

Since we'd left my house in Los Angeles at four A.M., it was still cool when we arrived here in the wilderness many hours later.

Together, my friend and I walk to the top of the tallest accessible hill, the place where I was to construct the medicine wheel. She then leaves, rattling her keys while she walks to scare off any rattlesnakes that might be lying in the thick dense grasses.

My dogs stay with me, curious about my activities as I gather large stones and lay out little bundles. This is to be a ceremony to the Spirits of Place, a ceremony for gathering power against harm.

I'd never done anything like this before, never seen anyone else perform such a ceremony either, so I proceed slowly, carefully and with great respect.

Rattlesnakes are one of the creatures I do not want to see today. I don't know quite how to ensure myself except to think positively and take my Kachina guard doll with the snakes around its neck into the circle with me. It is a Hopi Kachina flatdoll, "Sitihili" known as the rattlesnake Kachina, a guard Kachina in the Bear Dance ceremonies. He came to me in Sedona and I brought him home, not knowing that almost a year later I would need him for my own ceremony.

Surrounded by incense, candle, corn meal, tobacco, my

sacred bundle, sweet grass smudge stick, flowers, my rattles and the wilderness itself, sitting inside the medicine wheel with little wooden "Situlili," I begin to seek the spirits of place in the early morning.

Time seems to have stopped for me on that mountaintop. At moments I am shaken by the new information, moved to tears by the insights, awed by the power I feel around me, inside me, through me. The ancient spirits of place come from the six directions and share much wisdom with my own spirit.

At the very end, when the ritual has been completed but I am still sitting inside the medicine wheel, a last spirit appears. It is the spirit of "my own death" arriving on a sudden blast of wind. The spirit says it is angry with me because I left it behind when the spirit thought we'd become friends.

I tell the spirit of my own death that I will always bring it along with me now and that I understand the importance.

This teaching has to do with *fear*. If I bring my own death along with me as my friend, there is no other fear.

It is our new agreement.

I thank my own death and all the other spirits again. I ask them to protect this land which has healed and loved me from any harm that might come to it.

Nearly four hours after it began the ceremony is finished.

Everything from the ceremony is left in place. I take away only my brightly painted rattles from Cartegena, the Kachina, and my blanket.

The dogs and I walk down to the car where my friend has patiently waited. We all drive back to Los Angeles that same day in near silence.

Less than one month later, in a complex set of paperwork

transactions, the bank released me from past obligations. Then my interest in the ranch itself was sold for an all-cash payment. I was extricated from all the financial burden, set free from the emotional struggle and released from the people who intended me harm.

MAPMAKER

So, where am I—now?

In this kaleidoscopic journey of changing visions, versions of life's reality is ever challenging. This journey is the beginning of becoming a maker of maps.

The opportunities for personal transformation are seemingly endless.

What has been clear ever since my stroke in August 1981 is that none of my old habits, thoughts, attitudes, dreams or assumptions about who I am or how the world is were a suitable basis for continuing the journey of my life.

In addition, I needed to learn the concept of acceptance from a fundamental, experiential, everyday existence.

The first acceptance was that of life itself, the continuing opportunity *to be*.

However, "being" in the state I found myself—my body half paralyzed, unable to think or speak—was the second step of acceptance, a more difficult one by far than the fact I was still alive. Life or death did not seem to be under my control, so my acceptance of that outcome was a little easier.

After the stroke, being me, a physically handicapped and mentally impaired woman of forty-two, was a considerably more painful acceptance. That acceptance was intended, as I see it now through hindsight, to dissolve false ego, false pride, false sense of superiority—all products of a brutal childhood, which I thought had been necessary for survival. As these qualities I had previously looked upon as part of my self-esteem fell away, peeled off almost forcibly by the conditions of paralysis and brain damage, I could actually feel the stripping process as a series of physical/emotional events. Since my head had also been shaved in the hospital, the strange nakedness which greeted my eyes as I looked at my face in the mirror each day became symbolic of the greater nakedness of my soul, my inner spirit.

Cocooned for many months in a severely dysfunctional body, that inner spirit learned of a silence which was un-imaginable to me before. My inability to communicate with the world turned my thoughts inward, directing them to-ward my heart and my soul.

And, there were moments of terror. Everything familiar had failed me—my body, my mind, my world.

Strange sensations gripped me, such as hearing my own blood, seeing wholeness in my useless hand, imagining my-self capable and well but feeling faint and overwhelmed at the smallest external stimulation.

Unable to make any concrete decisions, my course became a venture into images, sounds, tastes, smells, the tiniest sen-sations. The nebulous, the invisible, the intangible were often the only avenues still open to me.

Yet always a constant companion was the need for me to learn, to accept. To accept each day as complete, to accept that day's small progress as what was possible and to find in my heart enough of that acceptance to also feel some gratitude.

Finally, my two years' walking alone in the wilderness with the dogs and working in my garden close to the earth strengthened my body, spiritually attuned my mind to understand my new connection to the universe.

Where I had been used to seeing the world as a confrontation, now my course was to learn trust in the quality of the universe itself. To learn to trust that I would be taken care of as long as I continued to follow the path of the heart and listened to the messages of the inner spirit. What began to emerge, after the very painful and confusing clearing process, was a new life.

This new life had a different experience of the world, a different understanding of what was important and what was not, a different perspective about self and others.

This new me reads lots of books on religion, metaphysics, history, healing and ancient traditions, which give me access to ancient knowledge and other forms of consciousness. This new me takes weekly yoga classes and studies Tai Chi.

This new me reaches out to new others, and reaches out and reaches out, learning as the process continues.

This new me becomes attuned to insights about life as it unfolds on a practical, everyday basis.

I had to find new friends, new avenues of expression, new sources of income, new ways of being in the world.

In fact, figuring out "what was" from "what was not" became almost a game.

For instance, if I looked at the calendar and saw that I had neither social nor business engagements for periods of time, was that to be called "emptiness" or "freedom"?

For instance, when I am by myself, is it called "isolation" or "connection"?

And when I face a month without work, is it faced with panic or with a sense of creative possibility?

What is it? It is my choice. I can call it emptiness or I can call it freedom.

So now, anytime I'm involved with struggle, I know that it's probably because I don't know how to see it or do it differently.

It's not a mistake. It's not a failure. It is just different.

And so, this is how I now live my life: carrying the child in my heart, reaching out as best I can, knowing that I am responsible for all of the choices, that my guidance comes from that quiet place deep within and that for me, acceptance has been a powerful key to unlock unlimited possibilities. Ultimately life all happens today and it only happens today.

So when I feel fragile and unsure, I go through my little checklist: do I have a place to live today? Do I have food today? Do I have money today? Am I well today? Most days, the answers are all "yes." If there are any "no's," then I do my best to deal with them specifically, and leave the "yes" answers peacefully aside until another today when they will be answered again.

Of course, I have goals and I've always had dreams. Each day I do my best to make them come true.

The way of the initiate is a journey well understood in ancient times but a difficult one to pursue in our modern Western world.

In Egypt even the ritual of resurrection was practiced on a regular basis. Initiates would be entombed for three days to contemplate the meaning of life, death and their individual journey through each. At the end of three days the tomb would be opened and a greatly enlightened initiate would reappear. The Indian tribes sent a young person into the wilderness for several days, alone and naked with only a blanket and a sacred ceremonial pipe to make their personal vision quest.

Today this kind of information is somewhat scattered. It is hard to sort through and sift the reputable from the fringe.

The difficulty is that at the moment, becoming an initiate has not yet achieved validation in our present culture. So the initiate, the person embarked on a journey of the soul, has no defined position as he or she tries to take a rightful place connected to the power of the universe.

That is why, it now seems to me, finding your own intuition, your own inner voice and paying close attention to the clues it gives you is so vitally important.

I believe all of us are given intuition. In the same way we all have eyes, but some people have the gift of creating art. We all have ears, but some create music. We all have legs, but some develop great athletic skill. We all have arms but some devise magical feats. We all have brains, but some perform miracles.

So far on this extraordinary journey, I have read a lot of different books, learned from religion, metaphysics, Buddhism, American Indians, the shamans and, I believe, from the universe itself.

Some powerful teachers have been sent to me from whom I have been privileged to learn in several different realities.

And I am sure this is just the beginning. I am still an initiate.

One thing I know is that it doesn't matter how you get on the path, whether you come through personal disillusionment with your current process, or whether you come through a near-death experience such as I had. It doesn't matter whether you jump on the journey like joining a circus bandwagon, or crawl onto the path fighting demons of drug and alcohol addiction.

None of that matters. The form doesn't matter. The way you get here is immaterial.

Once you arrive it also doesn't matter whether you're attracted to the "Course in Miracles" or the medicine wheel or healing crystals or past life regression. The form doesn't matter.

What matters is that you understand that the search is within you, that the journey you are on is within, not without.

Information may be sought anywhere you want. True answers will come only from within yourself, no matter how many healers or channels or psychics or teachers you see.

I now understand that no learning that makes a difference to my soul's evolutionary journey will come from outside.

Everything I need is inside, as soon as I made my connection with the universe, when I joined hearts.

When one is ready, when we chose, the understanding will be a part of life. Then we are guided very differently. At least, that's how it is for me.

I hardly recognize the person I was in the past because I bear so little resemblance to her today.

Finally, I am learning love. As long as I stay centered on that, it makes no difference to me how people judge me from the past.

The past is gone. It is now always today.

A MOMENT
IN TIME

THESE THOUGHTS CAME to me at the end of a two-week workshop at Esalen, Big Sur, California, in February 1988. They are, perhaps, the conclusion of my travels out of a place called Lost and the beginning of a new journey.

There is another place called A Moment in Time. If you will give us a moment in your time, I will show you a secret space, an opening where love slips through, where passion has no anger, where dreams come true.

In that secret space of time, I will kiss the inside of your smile. Not with my mouth, but through my heart, as we share a journey to the stars.

Seeing worlds we always dreamed, through an eternity bringing us here to this now time between us, before us.

In this time of now, in the space of a secret opening, you show me a face of always, behind the smile. Inside that smile is the fire, the women and men of trust. Outside the smile's protection is the still-grieving world.

So, I promise to kiss you there, inside your smile . . . inside the secret opening ... through this moment in time.

Yet, also in the journey we share to the outer limits, to the edge of the stars.

And, perhaps, as eternity herself smiles on us both, on us all ... we carry in our hearts—this moment in time!

BE HAPPY
LIVE WELL
HONOR THE JOY
YOU ALREADY KNOW

ACKNOWLEDGMENTS

Many people have helped along the way and I am specially grateful to them all. Richard Heller, my attorney, and Susan Schwartz, my editor. Friends and associates: Jane Cee Redbord; Mell Lazarus; Deanne Tilton; Milton Heifetz, M.D.; Sharon Berman; Glenn Redbord, Esq.; Alyssum Long; Barbara Hayes, Ph.D.; Roland Summit, M.D.; Richard Sutphen; Michael Harner, Ph.D.; Sandra Ingerman; Michael Durfee, M.D.; Gary Bostwick, Esq.; Lloyd Battista; Alice Miller, Ph.D.; Frank Fusina; Tom Rothman; Phillip and Roz Terry. Also, C. David Koontz and his son, David, who shared many of these years with me.

Organizations mentioned in this book may be contacted directly at the following address:

FOUNDATION FOR SHAMANIC STUDIES
Box 670, Belden Station
Norwalk, CT 06852

INSTITUTE OF NOETIC SCIENCES
475 Gate Five Road, Suite 300
P.O. Box 97
Sausalito, CA 94966-0097

RICHARD SUTPHEN
Sutphen Seminars/Valley of the Sun Publishing
Box 38
Malibu, CA 90265

SURVIVORS NETWORK
18653 Ventura Blvd., #143
Tarzana, CA 91356